THE BOUNDARIES OF THE ACCOUNTING UNIVERSE

This is a volume in the Arno Press collection

THE DEVELOPMENT OF CONTEMPORARY ACCOUNTING THOUGHT

See last pages of this volume for a complete list of titles.

THE BOUNDARIES OF THE ACCOUNTING UNIVERSE

George H. Sorter

ARNO PRESS
A New York Times Company
New York • 1978

Editorial Supervision: LUCILLE MAIORCA

First publication 1978 by Arno Press Inc.

THE DEVELOPMENT OF CONTEMPORARY ACCOUNTING THOUGHT
ISBN for complete set: 0-405-10891-5
See last pages of this volume for titles.

Manufactured in the United States of America

Library of Congress Cataloging in Publication Data

Sorter, George H.
The boundaries of the accounting universe.

(The Development of contemporary accounting thought)
Originally presented as the author's thesis, University of Chicago, 1963.
Bibliography: p.
1. Accounting. I. Title. II. Series.
HF5635.S715 1978 657 77-87308
ISBN 0-405-10947-4

THE BOUNDARIES OF THE ACCOUNTING UNIVERSE

THE ACCOUNTING RULES OF SELECTION

by

GEORGE H. SORTER

TO: William J. Vatter: The Father of this book and of my ideas.

PREFACE

AND

ACKNOWLEDGMENTS

This dissertation saw the light of day almost fifteen years ago. Surprisingly, however, the rules of selection identified in the paper continue to enforce with a sufficient degree of validity that no update was thought necessary. The author, after a painful rereading, would have loved to change the style of writing but that was not considered cricket.

To acknowledge all who aided the development of this paper would be impossible; not to acknowledge those listed below would be criminal. My sincere thanks go to:

- William J. Vatter, Sidney Davidson and James H. Lorie, the members of my thesis committee who gave generously of their time, their effort and their genius;
- Jacob Birnberg, David Drake, Nicholas Dopuch, David Green, Jr. Charles T. Horngren, Samuel Laimon and all members of the Workship in Accounting Research, of the Institute of Professional Accounting at the Graduate School of Business, University of Chicago, who listened and helped patiently and endlessly;
- Arthur Andersen and Co., who supported parts of this work financially and otherwise;
- Raymonde Rousselot who with rare cryptographic skill deciphered my hieroglyphics over the long period of seven years always with unfailing good nature, exemplary skill and utter dedication.

TABLE OF CONTENTS

LIST OF TABLES

INTRODUCTION

Accounting has long searched for a coherent and logical theory explaining and codifying existing accounting practices. So far this search has proved fruitless. As long ago as 1925 Yntema remarked:

> We have to face such problems as the measurement of various classes of business capital, the statement of income, and the calculation of the costs of securing that income, which I submit, are not problems to be passed by with the glib turn of an accounting axiom. It would seem that to deal properly with these questions, the rules of thumb should be subjected to close scrutiny, that their origin, their scope, their limitations and their validity should be carefully examined. I do not question the usefulness of working rules, for they will be necessary as long as there is work to be done. But it is not possible to explain these working rules, to construct a rational theory to which they will be related, which will serve as a guide in the adoption of new working rules as new exigencies force themselves upon us the problems to be solved change their complexion? [1]

Since then there has been a great deal of ferment in accounting, culminating in the innumerable current projects dealing with new accounting postulates, new basic principles of accounting, new accounting structures, and searching reappraisals of everything that has gone before.

Accounting theory has produced almost everything except that "close scrutiny" suggested by Yntema almost forty years ago.

Behavior must be understood before it can be changed. Before discarding what now exists, current practice must be analyzed, the rules and practices must be defined and stated in operational terms, and the rationale and logical structure of accounting must be carefully examined.

An important step in creating the new is an appreciation and understanding

---

[1] Theodore O. Yntema, "Discussion of Literature," Publication of The American Association of University Instructors in Accounting, IX, No. 1 (February, 1925), 62. Emphasis supplied.

of the old, and that understanding accounting has so far failed to develop. True, much as been said, written and argued about what accounting "principles" are,but no one has systematically examined what accounting really does. Einstein once advised: "Don't listen to their words, fix their attention on their deeds."[1] The aim of this paper is to fix attention on what accounting does. The paper will provide a "close scrutiny" of part of the accounting function -- the selection of the events to be recorded. Accounting is an information system and like any information system consists of three functions: selection, description, and communication of the subject matter. Accounting could deal with an almost infinite number of events. From these myriad possible events, those that form the subject matter of accounting must be selected. Once the events have been selected they must be described and finally communicated. To describe the behavior of the accounting system exhaustively, all three accounting functions must be analyzed, but such a task is clearly beyond the scope of a single work. The present study is limited to an analysis of the selection function. The implied rules of selection are stated in operational terms, and an attempt is made to isolate the logical relationship existing among these rules.

In general, the paper deals only with what is actually being done rather than what should be done, except that on some occasions the writer's zeal proved uncontainable. It is felt that a logical exposition of existing practice is a necessary, but often lacking, precedent to normative judgments.

Eighteen rules ofselection are derived in the paper. These eighteen rules exhaustively describe all of accepted accounting procedures in the area of selection. The recognition or nonrecognition of any accounting event is

---

[1] Quoted in Karl Pearson, The Grammar of Science (New York: The Meridian Books, Inc., 1957), p. v.

governed by one or more of these eighteen rules. Despite the diversity of accounting practice, it seems that accounting is pretty compact after all.

In order to derive and analyze these eighteen rules, chapter i defines the subject matter of accounting and presents a brief description of the description and communication function of accounting. Chapter ii is concerned with the construction of an organizational framework for potential accounting events and distinguishes between classes and categories of events. Chapter iii describes some of the problems encountered in assigning accounting events to specific classes and categories. In chapter iv, the one rule applicable to all events and the seven rules applicable to classes of events are presented. The ten rules applicable to categories of events are derived in chapter v. These eighteen rules are then carefully examined in chapter vi by analyzing current practice for each of the 125 possible events. This examination is undertaken to show that the rules correctly reflect current selection practice and that they explain *all* of current standard practices.

The concluding chapter presents a brief discussion of the apparent influence of auditability upon the selection rules, and suggests some of the potential benefits of the preceding analysis.

CHAPTER I

THE SUBJECT MATTER OF ACCOUNTING

Accounting has been variously defined as:

> . . . the art of recording, classifying and summarizing in a significant manner and in terms of money, transactions and events which are in part at least of a financial character, and interpreting the results thereof.[1]

> . . . the body of principles and the technichal mechanism by means of which the economic data of the particular concern are classified, recorded and periodically presented and interpreted.[2]

> . . . a device for measuring and interpreting certain quantatively expressed facts of an enterprise.[3]

A thread common to all of these definitions is that accounting is concerned with economic events. As a working provisional definition for the purposes of this paper, the subject matter of accounting is defined as "relevant economic events affecting an accounting unit." The purpose of accounting is therefore the communication of these relevant economic events to interested parties.

Several implications of this definition deserve brief comment. The definition implies that the subject matter of accounting is flexible since relevant events may differ from day to day or between accounting units. The definition also is nonrestrictive in the sense that the relevance of any given

---

[1] American Institute of Certified Public Accountants, Review and Resumé Bulletin, No. 1 (New York: American Institute of Certified Public Accountants, 1953), p. 9.

[2] W.A. Paton, Essentials of Accounting (New York: The Macmillan Company, 1938), p. 3.

[3] C. Rufus Rorem, Accounting Method (Chicago: University of Chicago Press, 1930), p. 3.

event does not imply the irrelevance of a different event. For example, an event establishing the cost of an item may be relevant, and events producing value changes in the same item may also be relevant. The recognition of one event does not affect the recognition or non-recognition of another event.

The definition does pose two questions: (1) what is the accounting unit? and (2) what are relevant events?

The answer to the first question has aroused a great deal of controversy in accounting theory. The accounting unit has variously been defined as a "proprietorship," and "entity" and a "fund."[1]

Although this controversy is of considerable interest, the definition of the accounting unit does not create any difficulties in delineating the subject matter of accounting. The accounting units need only be defined with sufficient precision so that it is possible to determine whether or not a given event produces an effect upon the unit. The three definitions of the accounting unit are similar enough so that the events producing an effect are the same whether the accounting unit is thought of as a fund, an entity, or a proprietorship.

What are the relevant events? The answer that current accounting practice supplies to that question provides the content of this work. The paper deals with the derivation and exposition of the selection rules implied by current practice. It must be emphasized that the concern here is with what the rules actually are, and not with what they should be, or with what they might become.

Before accounting practice in the area of selection can be identified, organized and described, a brief survey of the other accounting functions is

---

[1] For a good discussion of the three viewpoints, see William J. Vatter, The Fund Theory of Accounting and Its Implication for Financial Reports (Chicago: University of Chicago Press, 1947), chapter i.

essential. Accounting selects and then describes events in order to accomplish its purpose of communicating the relevant events. To understand selection, the description and communication processes need to be understood. They are described in this chapter.

Accounting Description

Accounting describes events by using both names and numbers. The prevalent method of accounting -- double entry accounting -- uses a minimum of two names and two numbers to describe each event. Each time an event is described, a classification decision (what name to use) must be made. It is interesting to take a closer look at the accounting names and numbers.

Accounting names

Every name used in accounting belongs either directly or indirectly to one of two groups -- assets or equities.[1]

Assets -- Currently there is substantial agreement in accounting that assets are best defined as "service potential."[2] The two requisites for an item of accountability to be classified as an asset are that the item produce service and that this service take place in the future. Since the future is involved, uncertainty rears its ugly head and some assumptions about the uncertain future must be included to make the "service potential" definition.

---

[1] Thus in nonincome related events both names used to describe the event fall directly into the asset-equity categories. In income related events, one of the names used is an asset or equity, the other is included in the equity category by implication.

[2] See for instance, American Accounting Association, Accounting and Reporting Standards for Corporate Financial Statements and Preceding Statements and Supplements (Columbus: American Accounting Association, 1957), p. 3. Vatter, p. 17. This is not a new notion, for Canning in 1929 termed assets as "Future Service," John B. Canning, The Economics of Accounting (New York: The Ronald Press Company, 1929), p. 12. For the evolution of the definitions of asset, see David Green, Jr., "A Moral to the Direct Costing Controversy?" The Journal of Business, XXXIII (July, 1960), 218-26.

operational. Clearly the asset category would be quite different if atomic war were forecast for tomorrow, rather than say utopia. Given each of the possible general futures, the probability of service for each particular item can be anywhere between 0.00 and 1.00. The "service potential" definition is mute whether an item shall be termed an asset only if the probability of service is 1.00 for <u>any</u> possible future or whether all items having a 0.01 probability of yielding service in <u>a</u> possible future may be included in the asset category.

Two kinds of uncertainty affect the definition of an asset: (1) uncertainty about the general future facing the accounting unit and (2) uncertainty about the service to be expected from each item, given a general future. In a sense, these two problems can be reduced to one. If it were possible to calculate the probability of each general future occurring, and then calculate the probability of each item possessing service potential, the produce of these probabilities would provide the probability of service potential for each item. Only if the probability exceeded "X" would the item be classified as an asset.

A more manageable approach is to accept the most probable future as given and within <u>that</u> future specify a threshold probability. Only items for which the porbability of service potential exceeded the threshold probability would qualify as assets. Though these probabilities defy precise numerical quantification, it is possible to attempt a comparative quantification, i.e., the probability of expenditures for research possessing service potential is less than the probability of plant expenditures yielding service, but larger than the probability that service will result from contributions to the Community Fund.

Despite the obvious difficulties involved, such problems do not disappear if they are ignored. Assumptions as to the probability for service potential must be made in justifying the rational inclusion or exclusion of items in the asset category and therefore are necessary for an operational definition of assets.

Tentatively assets are defined as "any item possessing a specified minimum probability of yielding future service, assuming the most probable general future as given."

Equities -- Turning to the other main group of accounting names, equities, no concensus about the proper definition of the term can be found. In fact, there is no agreement as to the proper name for this gourp. Some call the group "equities," others "liabilities" and still others "liabilities and net worth." Some define "the other group" as "claims,"[1] others feel that they should be thought of as "sources"[2] and Vatter defines equities as "restrictions."[3] All three of these definitions appear faulty. Equities are here defined as "any item possessing a certain minimum probability of imposing a responsibility upon the accounting unit." Equities are defined as responsibilities.

Most authorities accept the definition of equities as claims. Webster defines a claim as "A demand for something rightfully or allegedly due; assertion of one's right to something."[4] Most equities in no way represent a current clear demand or an assertion of rights. Further, if the claim definition is valid, the differentiation between equities that are currently found in accounting ought to be explainable by the different nature of the claims. This is not so. "The claim of the stockholder whenever it does come into the field

---

[1] American Accounting Association, p. 7.

[2] For an excellent discussion of the arguments for equities as sources see David Green, Jr., "Accounting for Corporate Retained Earnings" (unpublished Ph.D. dissertation, Graduate School of Business, University of Chicago, 1956), pp. 17-20.

[3] Vatter, p. 19.

[4] Webster's New Collegiate Dictionary (Springfield, Mass.: G. & C. Merriam Co., 1958), p. 151.

of legal significance, is not fundamentally different with respect to the items classified as capital stock, capital surplus, appropriated or unappropriated earned suprlus."[1] Finally, the word claim has an active relationship to the person holding the claim and only a passive relationship to the accounting unit against which the claim is held. It is almost as if claims more directly describe the person holding the claim rather than the accounting unit. Since equities are one of the two groups of names used by accounting to describe the accounting unit and its actions, it is appropriate to define equities through an active and direct relationship to the unit.

Instead of defining equities as claims, it has been suggested that equities should be defined as "Sources of assets." Source of assets seems to provide a useful but incomplete description of equities. For example, "bonds payable" does suggest that a certain amount of assets were supplied by a particular group of creditors, but it suggests more than that. It suggests, for instance, that a certain amount of interest and principle is to be paid. Not only is source an incomplete description of equities, but it is not operational. What sources do taxes payable represent? How is one source distinguished from another? What distinguished the creditor and owner? The creditor and owner are distinguished by the different responsibilities their contributions impose upon the accounting unit. In other words, the source of assets is really operationally defined by the responsibilities the firm assumes in exchange for the assets received.

The definition of equities as restrictions is superior to the two definitions so far discussed. But restriction implies a precise restraint that many equities just do not impose. It seems to be stretching a point to maintain

---

[1] Vatter, p. 19.

that "contributed capital" or "common stock" impose any formal restriction on the firm.[1]

Needed is a definition of equities that focuses attention on the accounting unit; that implies the notion of source and that explains the differences between equities. Defining equities as responsibilities accomplishes this. Equities are the responsibilities of the accounting unit; these responsibilities are directed toward someone and therefore imply a source. The existing differences in equities can be explained by the different responsibilities implied.

Liabilities represent responsibilities of precise dollar amounts, that must be met in a prescribed manner, at a prescribed time. Common stock on the other hand represents an open ended responsibility incapable of precise quantification. Nevertheless the entity does assume a specific responsibility when a share of stock is issued. The firm is now committed to a course of action that it was not committed to previously. The firm must allow the holder of the share a voice in management, and must allow him to share in the profits of the enterprise.

Contrast the specific responsibilities implied by liabilities and common stock with the responsibility implied by retained earnings. Retained earnings represent the responsibilities created by the net asset inflow from operations. The accounting unit does not undertake any new commitments in exchange for the assets generated by customers. These assets do not commit the enterprise to a specific course of action to whichthe enterprise was not previously committed. The enterprise is, of course, responsible for these assets as it is for all assets. But this responsibility is of a completely general nature, namely that the assets must be used lawfully and in conformity with the

---

[1] See Green, "Accounting for Corporate Retained Earnings," p. 19.

corporate charter. The responsibilities created by liabilities and contributed capital are here defined as specific responsibilities. The responsibility implied b the retained earnings account is defined as the residual responsibility.

Both assets and equities possess two dimensions, a quantity dimension and a time dimension. The quantity dimension describes the amount of service or responsibility to be expected or demanded, while the time dimension describes when the service or responsibility is to be rendered.

Accounting numbers

Only one unit of quantification is used by accounting -- the official unit of currency. In the United States, all accounting quantifications represent dollars. As already mentioned, double entry accounting utilizes at lease two numbers to describe each event. Attached to each accounting number is one of two accounting signs termed "debit" and "credit." The sume of debits must equal the sum of credits for each event.

Accounting Communication

Accounting uses two forms of formal communication. All events are communicated indirectly by reporting the effect the events have on the specific assets and equities. This communication is achieved through the balance sheet which reports the balances of assets and equities existing at a moment of time. These balances represent the cumulative net effect of all the events that have occurred since the inception of the accounting unit, upon the given categories. In a sense, the balance sheet represents an indirect communication of all the events since inception of the unit. If only the balances are reported, the events themselves are submerged. True, the effects of the events are reported, but many different combinations of events could have produced the same effects.

Some events of particular importance are communicated directly through an organized listing of the events themselves. This direct and dynamic reporting can be accomplished through such flow reports as the fund statement, the cash receipts and disbursement statement and similar reports. At present the only mandatory flow report consists of the income statement. Thus, events having an income effect (however defined) must be summarized and reported directly through the income statement as well as indirectly through the balance sheet.

Conclusion

In this chapter the subject matter of accounting was defined as relevant economic events. The accounting functions of description and communication were briefly described, and assets and equities, the classes of accounting names were defined as service potential and responsibilities, respectively. This sets the stage for chapter ii where an organization framework for accounting events is presented.

CHAPTER II

ACCOUNTING CLASSES AND CATEGORIES

In this chapter a framework is developed for organizing all the possible events that might be recognized by the accounting process. Such a framework is essential for the systematic analysis of the selection rules. The framework developed is based on two criteria -- cause and effect. While any organizational scheme is necessarily arbitrary, this particular framework and the particular causes and effects are used for several reasons. First, all accounting events, as indeed all events,must be initiated by a cuase or stimulus, and must produce an observable effect or response. Therefore, each accounting effect will fit into such a framework. Secondly, although an accounting event may proceed from more than one cause and produce more than one effect, these compound events can be expressed as sums of events,each with only one cause and one effect. Therefore, each accounting event can be so defined that it will fit into only one niche of the framework. The classification, as a result, is both exhaustive and exclusive. Thirdly, the framework yields groupings to which identical rules of selection apply. In general, the same rule applies to events of one group and different rules apply to members of different groups.

The different groupings produced by the taxonomical scheme used are defined below. These definitions are arbitrary but help in the exposition of what is to come.

A _class_ prepresents a grouping by cause; a _category_ is a grouping by effect and a _type_ is a grouping by both cause and effect. The different classes and categories actually used in this study are defined and examined in the remainder of this chapter.

Classes of Events

The following five classes of events are used in this study: (1) market transactions, (2) general changes, (3) specific changes, (4) forecase changes, and (5) conversions. It would have been perfectly possible to use more or less than five classes of events or to use a different set of five classes. The arbitrary decision to use these particular five classes was made because different rules apply to different classes. The classes are defined in the next paragraphs.

Market Transactions: A market transaction is an event originated by the voluntary interaction between the accounting unit and some other unit. -- An event, in order to be classified as a market transaction must be voluntary and must involve an entity besides the accounting unit. Thefts and embezzlements would not qualify as market transactions because they are not voluntary interactions; the conversion of work in process into finished goods would not qualify because no other entity is directly involved in the event. Voluntary exchanges of money, goods, services and promises are all classified as market transactions.

General Changes: An event occasioned by a change in the general environment affecting all accounting units. -- A change in the general price level represents an event of this class. These changes produce a direct impact upon the dollar and since the dollar is the quantification measure used by all accounting units, these events necessarily affect all possible accounting units.

Specific Changes: A change in the environment, not affecting all accounting units, but having a particular effect upon the given accounting unit. -- All changes in the environment producing an economic effect on one or some (but not all) units belong to this class of events. This economic change may or may not be accompanied by a change in physical or legal conditions. A change in the price of a specific kind of asset used by a firm is such an event unaccompanied by physical or legal changes. Another purely economic change is a change in the demand schedule for a product produced by the firm. Both these events are specific rather than general changes, since the event has significance only for firms using the particular asset, or producing the particular product. A fire destroying or damaging some of the assets of the accounting unit represents a specific change in both the physical and economic environment and the expiration of a contract produces both economic and legal changes. All of these events are considered specific changes.

Forecast Changes: An event occasioned by a changed forecast. -- First, it must be noted that the forecast itself is part of the past and not the future. True, the forecast deals with the future, but it is made in the present, and once made, becomes just as much a part of the history of the accounting unit as the purchase of inventory or the production of steel. Including forecasts as potential accounting events is therefore completely consistent with the notion of accounting as history.

Accounting forecasts must deal with forecasts related to the basic accounting concepts of assets and equities. As discussed in chapter i, both assets and equities have a quantity dimension, i.e., how much service is expected and how much the responsibility consists of. Assets and equities also have a time or duration dimension that describes when and over what period service is expected and responsibility demanded. Forecasts may be made about either the quantity or time dimension of an asset and equity. Paradoxically, the time dimension need not always be described by units of time. A man's life span (time dimension) may be specified as 60 years, but it may also be described as 1,866,240,000 heartbeats. An asset's life span may be described as either ten years, or say 10,000 machine hours. Either description describes the time span over which service may be expected. It is important to distinguish between forecasts about the quantity and time dimensions since accounting rules treat these forecasts differently.

Forecasts about the life span or time dimension of assets and equities need to be further broken down into absolute and relative forecast changes. An absolute change represents a new forecast due to changed expectations about the time span itself. A relative change represents a new forecast due to the movement in time of the forecaster in relation to an unchanged expectation about the time span. An example may be needed to clarify this distinction. Suppose that based on present actuarial knowledge, men of both age 21 and 22 have the same probability, say 78, of attaining age 65. Then a 21-year-old male may express this forecast in absolute terms as follows: "I have a 78 per cent chance of attaining age 65." On his 22nd birthday, this statement would continue to be true. There has been no absolute change in his forecast. Actually, this absolute forecase was given in its most simple form, it could have been expressed more completely as "I have a 78 per cent chance to attain age 65 at ages 21 and 22, a 79 per cent change to attain age 65 if I live to age 23, etc. etc." This forecast would continue to remain valid till age 65, in the absence of a change in probabilities. The 21-year-old male, however, could have stated his life expectancy in a relative way as follows: "I have a 78 per cent chance of living for at least 44 more years"; this statement would no longer be true on his 22nd birthday; he would now say: "I have a 78 per cent chance to live for at least 43 more years." There has been a relative, but not an absolute, change in forecasts during the year. Some would argue that the latter change does not represent a changed forecast at all -- it certainly is different from an absolute change. It further is a predictable change. However, if a forecast about a time span expresses a relationship between the forecaster and the future, a change can be said to occur either when expectations about the future change, or when the forecasters position in time relative to an unchanged future changes.

The situation is analogous to the difference between a movement along a demand curve and a shift of the demand curve. A given firm's demand curve indicates that at $1.00, 2 units will be demanded and at $2.00 only one unit will be demanded. If the price changes from $1.00 to $2.00 and the quantity demanded decreases from two to one, this is somewhat analogous to a relative forecast change. If the demand schedule actually shifts, this is analogous to an absolute forecast change.

Converstions: An event in which the accounting unit is the only entity directly involved. -- A conversion represents any event involving only the accounting unit. The best example of an event of this class is the manufacturing process.

Categories of Events

The grouping of events by effect yields categories of events. Four main categories and twenty-five subcategories are used in this paper. Since accounting describes the events by using two groups of names -- assets and equities, accounting events exclusively affect assets and equities. Under the principal of double entry, an event is always described by at least two names and two numbers. Furthermore, accounting attaches to each number used an "accounting sign," called "debit" or "credit," in such a manner that the sum of debits used to describe an event must be equal to the sum of credits used in describing the same event. The rules for attaching accounting signs are as follows:

An increase in assets = "debit"
A drecrease in assets = "credit"
An increase in equities = "credit"
A decrease in equities = "debit"

From these rules it follows that an accounting event increasing assets must always either decrease other assets, or increase equities; and an event increasing equities must decrease other equities or increase assets and vice versa. Therefore, four main categories of the effects of accounting events are immediately established.

I. Asset Increase / Equity Increase
II. Asset Decrease / Equity Decrease
III. Asset Increase / Asset Decrease
IV. Equity Increase / Equity Decrease

Within these four main categories it is useful to identify subcategories based upon the kind of assets and equities affected by the event.

Kind of assets

Assets need only have economic substance. Economic existence, a minimal expected value of service, is the only necessary attribute of an asset.

Properties possessing economic substance, may of course, also possess physical and/or legal substance. Economic existence is necessary, legal or physical existence is possible. It is perhaps not surprising that accounting differentiates between assets having a legal or physical existence as well as economic existence, and those that exist only in the economic realm. This suggests the subcategories of assets that are used here. Physical assets are those assets that possess physical as well as economic substance. Legal assets are those assets that possess legal as well as economic substance, and economic assets are those that only have economic substance. Somewhat arbitrarily cash is here considered a physical asset even though strictly speaking cash might more properly be considered a legal asset, or perhaps a unique asset by itself.

Accounting rules in general treat cash like a physical asset and rather than set up another subcategoryof assets, with cash the only member, cash is included in the physical asset category.

Kinds of equities

For purposes of categorization, equities are separated into two kinds. Specific equities are those that impose specific responsibilities upon the accounting unit; the residual equity imposes only a general responsibility upon the equity.

The Resulting Categories

Utilizing the kinds of assets and equities discussed above yields four main categories of events and twenty-five subcategories as follows:

I. Asset Increase / Equity Increase

1. Physical - Residual
2. Physical - Specific
3. Legal - Residual
4. Legal - Specific
5. Economic - Residual
6. Economic - Specific

II. Asset Decrease / Equity Decrease

7. Physical - Residual
8. Physical - Specific
9. Legal - Residual
10. Legal - Specific
11. Economic - Residual
12. Economic - Specific

III. Asset Increase / Asset Decrease

13. Physical - Physical
14. Physical - Legal
15. Physical - Economic
16. Legal - Physical
17. Legal - Legal
18. Legal - Economic
19. Economic - Physical
20. Economic - Legal
21. Economic - Economic

IV. Equity Increase / Equity Decrease

22. Specific - Residual
23. Specific - Specific
24. Residual - Specific
25. Residual - Residual

Types of Events

Multiplying the five classes of events with the twenty-five categories produces a combination of 125 types of events as seen in Table 1.

Conclusion

To facilitate the analysis of accounting events, an organizational framework for potential accounting events is highly desirable. In this paper, accounting events are arbitrarily grouped by two criteria: cause and effect. The groupings achieved by association through cause are defined as classes of events; the groupings obtained through ordering by effect are termed categories of events; and the combination of these, i.e. the grouping of events due to both cause and effect are defined as types of events. Five classes of events and twenty-five categories of events were defined yielding 125 types of events that will be analyzed in the subsequent chapters.

TABLE I

THE POTENTIAL ACCOUNTING UNIVERSE

Category	Class									
	Market Transactions		General Changes		Specific Changes		Forecast Changes		Conversion	
	A		B		C		D		E	
	Recorded	Rule	Recorded	Rule	Recorded	Rule	Recorded	Rule	Recorded	Rule
I. Asset Increase / Equity Increase										
1. Physical - Residual										
2. Physical - Specific										
3. Legal - Residual										
4. Legal - Specific										
5. Economic - Residual										
6. Economic - Specific										
II. Asset Decrease / Equity Decrease										
1. Physical - Residual										
2. Physical - Specific										
3. Legal - Residual										
4. Legal - Specific										

5. Economic - Residual										
6. Economic - Specific										

III. Asset Increase / Asset Decrease

1. Physical - Physical										
2. Physical - Legal										
3. Physical - Economic										
4. Legal - Physical										
5. Legal - Legal										
6. Legal - Economic										
7. Economic - Physical										
8. Economic - Legal										
9. Economic - Economic										

IV. Equity Increase / Equity Decrease

1. Specific - Residual										
2. Specific - Specific										
3. Residual - Specific										
4. Residual - Residual										

CHAPTER III

THE PROBLEMS OF CLASSIFICATION AND CATEGORIZATION

In the preceding chapter, a framework for grouping potential events was constructed. The task now becomes to assign the actual accounting events to classes and categories. Most events fit easily into the various classes and categories, but some events are more difficult to assign. This chapter examines the classification and categorization of these maverick events.

Problems of Classification

The events defying easy classification all concern the expiration of time and its effect on assets and equities. The classification of the following events is discussed below: (1) interest income, (2) interest charges, and (3) amortization.

Interest Income

Interest income is defined as the difference between the cost of the asset when it is acquired and the total amount of payment received over the lifespan of the asset. This difference may be received in the form of equal periodic payments as is that case when a bond is acquired at par. Alternatively, the interest may be received in a lump sum at the time the investment is liquidated. A savings bond is an example of the latter situation. Combinations of these two situations are also found in the case of bonds issued at a premium or discount. Regardless of when the payments are received, accounting income is recognized at intervals over the entire lifespan of the investment. In the periodic payment situation, the interest income is recorded periodically by the following entry:

(1) Dr. Interest Receivable
Cr. Interest Income

In the savings bond case, income is also recorded periodically, but by the following entry:

(2) Dr. Investment
Cr. Interest Income

For bonds issued at a premium or discount, interest is periodically recorded with the following entry:

(3) Dr. Interest Receivable
Dr. or Cr. Investment
Cr. Interest Income

For all three situations, and independent of the cash receipts, interest income is recorded periodically. The question is how to classify the recognition of interest income. Superficially it might appear that interest income represents a specific change increasing the investment held. This classification must be rejected. Interest income is recognized without regard to anything, or almost anything, that might actually have occurred in the environment. Thus the same amount of interest income will be recognized in each period, if the value of the investment increases or decreases; if the market rate of interest goes up or down. If the recognition of interest represented a specific change, these changes in value would surely affect the recording of income. The actual recognition of income is completely predictable and determined at the time the asset is acquired; this argues conclusively against the classification of interest income as a specific change.

Interest income represents a relative forecast change about the lifespan of the investment. What has occurred is that the accounting unit has moved in time relative to an unchanged forecast about the timing of the expected receipts. This type of event was defined as a relative forecast change in the previous chapter.[1]

An example might clarify this view. Assume that a two year $1,000, 6 per cent bond is bought at par. The asset acquired by the investor is the right to receive $60.00 one year hence, and $1,060 at the end of the second year. These amounts are specified and quantified by the market transaction. The aggregate receivable is $1,120. This receivable must be reduced by an amount describing the expected timing of the receipts. The amount reducing the aggregate receivable to the present value or cost of the investment, at the time of purchase, is termed a "forecast offset." The original purchase can then be described as follows:

Aggregate Receivable	1,120			
Forecast Offset	(120)	1,000		
			Cash	1,000

After one year, and just before the receipt of the first interest payment, the relative forecast has changed. The total amount of money to be received has not changed, and the absolute forecast has not changed. A year ago, the relative forecast called for the receipt of $60.00 one year from date, and $1.060 two years from date. Now the relative forecast states that $60.00 is expected immediately and $1,060 one year from now. This change can be recorded by the following entry:

Dr. Forecast Offset	60.00		
		Cr. Interest Income	60.00

and the balance sheet description of the investment would be as follows:

Aggregate Receivable	1,120	
Forecast Offset	(60)	1,060

The receipt of the interest payment would be recorded as:

Dr. Cash	60.00		
		Cr. Aggregate Receivable	60.00

and the new balance sheet representation would be:

---

[1] See the definition of relative vs. absolute forecast changes in chapter ii above.

Aggregate Receivable	1,060	
Forecast Offset	(60)	1,000

The question may well be raised, why all the rigamarole? Does not the interest income merely represent the change in the present value of the investment? The answer is that it does, only when there has been no change in interest rates. The recognition of interest income is unaffected by changes in interest rate; the present value of the investment is not. Ergo, interest income is not identical with present value changes. In the absence of interest rate changes, the change in present value does describe the movement of the accounting unit in time relative to the expected receipts, and it is this movement that is here described as a "relative forecast change."

Accepting the proposed description for the investment and for income recognition has several advantages. The primary advantage for this paper is that it clarifies the nature of the "interest income" event. It would also help answer the bothersome question as to why the par amount (to be received two years from now) is recognized as an asset when the investment is purchased, whereas the interest to be received one year from now is not recognized as an asset. The answer, of course, is that this only appears to be the case. By netting the aggregate receivable with the forecast offset, the par amount results, if the asset is purchased at par. This situation is clear if the investment is described as suggested above. The distinction between current and non-current assets could also be sharpened if the proposed description is adopted. The portion of the aggregate receivable -- the interest to be received one year from now and an appropriate amount of the "forecast offset," could be reported as current asset. Presently, the only portion of the aggregate receivable reported as a current asset is the amount of "interest receivable" accrued. The problem of how to report the "discount and premium" would disappear. A discount means nothing more than that the forecast offset is greater than the total interest to be received; a premium indicates that the forecast offset is less than the interest to be received.

The suggested description achieves exactly the same result as current practice. The difference is that originally the investment is described as the "aggregate receivable" and a corresponding "forecast offset" rather than a net amount. Subsequently, instead of recognizing "interest receivable," the suggested method would decrease the "forecast offset." At all times the "aggregate receivable" less the "forecast offset" would equal the "investment" plus "interest receivable" as it is currently reported. The proposed change is solely a descriptive change that has relevance for this paper only because it elucidates the nature of the interest income event. Interest income represents a relative change in forecasts.

Interest charges[1]

The recognition of an interest charge is an event of a similar type, but of opposite sign as the "interest income" event. The issue of a $1,000, 6 per cent, two-year loan at par is normally recorded as:

Dr. Cash	1,000.00			
		Cr. Loan Payable	1,000.00	

It can be described gross as

Dr. Cash	1,000.00			
		Cr. Aggregate Payable	1,120.00	
		Forecast Offset	(120.00)	1,000.00

The recognition of the interest charge represents the reduction of the offset. As time passes, the discharge of the responsibility becomes more imminent. This event represents a relative forecast change aboutthe time-span of the responsibility.

---

[1] The classification used here is essentially similar to the treatment recommended by Anton. See, Hector R. Anton, "Accounting for Bond Liabilities," The Journal of Accountancy, III, No. 3 (September, 1956), 53-56.

Amortization

The most difficult accounting events to classify are depreciation and other types of amortization. Many people have ideas on what depreciation should be, but few know what it represents as currently recorded by the accounting process. The major alternative to viewing dpereciation as a forecast change is to consider it a specific change in the depreciable asset, i.e., a change in value. Accounting does not consider it a value change or any change at all. The AICPA Committee on Terminology defines depreciation as follows:

> Depreciation accounting is a system of accounting which aims to distribute the cost or other basic value of tangible capital assets, less salvage (if any) over the estimated useful life of the unit (which may be a group of assets) in a systematic and rational manner. It is a process of allocation, not of valuation. Depreciation for the year is the protion of the total charge under such a system that is allocated to the year. Although the allocation may properly take into account occurrences during the year, it is not intended to be a measurement of the effect of all such occurrences.[1]

Preceding this definition is the following paragraph:

> Definitions are unacceptable which imply that depreciation for the year is a measurement, expressed in monetary terms, of the physical deterioration within the year, or of the decline in monetary value within the year, or, indeed of anything that actually occurs within the year. True, an occurrence within the year may justify or require a revision of prior estimates as to the length of useful life, but the annual charge remains an allocation to the year of a proportionate part of a total cost or loss estimated with reference to a longer period.[2]

These quotations emphatically reject the view that accounting depreciation represents a specific change. What is it then? Depreciation, like interest income and interest charge is a relative forecast change. At the time the asset is acquired, it is anticipated that it will last, say ten years. After one year of use, in conformity with the original forecast, the asset is expected to last 9 years. The depreciation charge represents this change in forecast. The

---

[1] American Institute of Certified Public Accountants, p. 25. Emphasis supplied.

[2] Ibid., pp. 24-25. Emphasis supplied.

similarity of this event to interest income and interest expense is obvious. All are relative changes occasioned by a movement in time of the accounting unit relative to an unchanged absolute forecast. Other amortizations represent similar forecast changes. "In the case of purchased goodwill, the most reasonable policy is to set up a schedule of amortization in harmony with the process of valuation employed in setting up the original charge."[1] The implication is that a forecast is made at the time of acquisition, and the subsequent amortization represents the "unwinding" of the original expectation. Depletion falls into this class of events and represents a relative change in forecasts. In this case, the forecast about the life span is expressed in units of product rather than units of use. If a mine was originally expected to yield 1,000 units, then, after mining 100 units, only 900 units are expected to be mined.

As discussed in chapter i, each asset (and equity) has a time dimension indicating when service (responsibility) is to be expected, and a quantity dimension indicating how much service (responsibility) is to be expected. The quantums of service may be discrete or continuous. In the case of interest bearing investments, the services, i.e., the expected receipts, are discrete. As the life span of the asset decreases, these concrete quantums of service become more immediate, and the relative forecast change results in an increased quantification of the asset.

The service provided by amortizable assets is generally continuous and as the life span decreases, the forecast changes in two ways. The remaining service becomes more immediate and results in an asset increase, but less total service is expected due to the smaller number of periods remaining. The change in forecasts is the difference between these and almost always will result in a net asset decrease.

---

[1] Rufus Wixon (ed.), Accountant's Handbook (4th ed.; New York: The Ronald Press Company, 1956), p. 19.17.

In each case, a forecast, about the life span of the asset or equity is formed at acquisition. As time passes, or units are produced, this forecast necessarily changes in a relative manner. This relative change in forecasts and its resultant effect upon the asset or equity involved is afforded accounting recognition, through the recording of interest, depreciation, depletion, and like events.

Problems of Categorization

The only events creating problems of categorization were certain exchanges and the events tradiationally described by accounting as "acquisition of expenses." These events are discussed below.

Exchanges

Described below are four exchanges of assets for which three different accounting treatments exist.

The exchange of cash for inventory, i.e., a purchase. -- This event is always recorded as a straight exchange, no equity is involved. The inventory purchased is always quantified by the outflowing cash, and the asset increase is therefore equal to the asset decrease. The entry is:

Dr. Inventory
Dr. Cash

The exchange of inventory for cash, i.e., a sale. -- In this case, accounting rules permit independent quantifications of the inflow and outflow and the residual equity may be affected. The quantification of the inflowing cash is obviously independent of the outflowing inventory. The quantification of the inventory is provided by existing accounting records. Many costs applicable to the sale are joint and cannot readily be identified at the point of sale nor assigned to a specific unit of product. For these reasons, accounting records the exchange as the sum of a separate inflow and outflow as follows:

The Inflow:

Dr. Cash

Cr. Sales

The Outflow:

(1) Dr. Cost of Goods Sold
Cr. Inventory — for the direct outflow

and

(2) Dr. Expenses
Cr. Miscellaneous Accounts — for the indirect outflow

Sales represent a residual equity increase and expenses represent a residual equity decrease. In this paper debits or credits to expense or revenue accounts are treated as debits or credits to the residual equity.

The sale of unusual and noncurrent assets such as capital assets or investments. -- Accounting permits an independent quantification of the inflow and outflow and an effect on the residual equity is poosible and likely. In this case the inflow and outflow are not recorded separately, but through a compound entry describing the exchange and the effect on the residual equity. The sale of an investment would be recorded by the following compound entry:

Dr. Cash
Dr. Residual Equity or Cr. Residual Equity
Cr. Investment

The exchange of accounts receivable for cash, i.e., collection from customers. -- In this case, accounting would probably permit an independent quantification of the inflow (cash) and the outflow (accounts receivable). The inflow and outflow would so rarely differ that the residual equity would almost never be involved. Accounting records this event as a simple asset increase/ asset decrease event as follows:

Dr. Cash

Cr. Accounts Receivable

Accounting describes these four events in three different ways. Events

1 and 4 are recorded as simple exchanges of assets, event 2 is described by two independent entries: as asset / residual equity increase and an asset / residual equity decrease, and event 3 is described by a compound entry -- reflecting the asset increase / asset decrease, and the residual equity increase or decrease.

For categorization purposes, it is cumbersome to have four exchanges treated in three different ways. Whenever accounting rules <u>permit</u> independent quantifications of the incoming and outgoing assets, and therefore permit a potential effect on the residual equity, the event will be treated as a combination of two distinct events -- an inflow and an outflow. Situations 2, 3 and 4 will all be described as follows:

(1) Dr. Asset
Cr. Residual Equity
for the inflow

(2) Dr. Residual Equity
Cr. Asset
for the outflow

The purchase of inventory, because accounting rules prohibit the independent quantification of the inflow and outflow, is the only one of the above events categorized as an "asset increase / asset decrease" event. The other three events will all be treated as the sum of two events:

Asset / Equity Increase and
Asset / Equity Decrease

<u>The purchase of expenses</u>

When services with extremely short life spans, yielding benefits of short duration are acquired, accounting often records both the acquisition and expiration of the service by one entry such as:

Dr. Labor Expense
Cr. Wages Payable

This entry describes an impossible event given rational economic action.

An expense is an "expired cost" and "expired costs are those having no discernable benefit to future operations." The above entry on the face of it represents the acquisition of something yielding no future benefit. This surely represents irrational behavior.

The entry really represents two events:

(1) The acquisition of the labor services

Dr. Labor Services

Cr. Wages Payable

and (2) The expiration of these services

Dr. Expense

Cr. Labor Services

Netting obscures the analysis and understanding of the underlying events. In this paper, these events will be recorded gross. Whenever services are acquired, an asset is created -- the right to the services. The performance of the service extinguishes this right. If the service results in future benefits, a conversion to another asset results. If these services do not yield future benefits either because they benefited the present, or because they were wasted, the final expiration of the asset is recorded. The acquisitions and thesubsequent dispositions of services should be recorded by the following entries:

(1) Dr. Services (an asset)

Cr. Payables

and by either one of these entries:

(2a) Dr. Asset

Cr. Services

or (2b) Dr. Expense

Cr. Services

Entry (1) records the acquisition, entry (2a) records the conversion or entry, (2b) records the expiration. In this paper, theseevents will be categorized and described in the above manner.

CHAPTER IV

THE CLASS RULES

In the preceding chapters the classes and categories of events were defined and the problems of assigning events to appropriate groups dealt with. In this and the following chapter, the selection rules applicable to the various classes and categories are derived. A rule is termed a class rule, if it applies to more than one category within a class. Rules applicable to only one category of a given class and rules applicable to more than one class are considered category rules. The category rules are discussed in chapter v. The one general rule and the seven class rules are the substance of this chapter.

The General Rule

One rule applies to all events and takes precedence over all other rules. It is:

Rule X: An event whose recognition is required or
sanctioned by a governmental agency may
be recorded

If something is acceptable to the Internal Revenue Service for tax purposes, it is acceptable to accounting for book purposes. If Congress says the distribution of General Motors stock to DuPont stockholders can be treated by the recipients as a return of capital, DuPont can, on its books, record the dividend as a dividend out of capital.

Class Rules

The following rules are applicable to the indicated classes. There are two rules applicable to market transactions; one rule each applies to general and specific changes; three rules apply to forecasts and no class rule exists for conversions.

Rules applicable to market transactions

A-1: All market transactions involving physical assets must be recorded

No event involving the receipt of disposal of a physical asset is unrecorded by the accounting process. This is true whether or not an accrual system of accounting is used. The accounting process does allow some latitude as to how such a market transaction shall be described. The quantification of the incoming asset may have to equal the quantification of the outgoing asset -- in which case no equity is involved. The inflow may be independent of the outflow in which case an equity may be involved. Howsoever such an event is described, it is always recognized. There are no events, where a physical asset is either received from or delivered to another unit, that remain unrecorded.

A-2: All market transactions decreasing legal assets must be recorded

Some market transactions, specifically certain contracts, remain unrecorded by accounting -- and no mandatory rule governing the recognition of legal asset increases resulting from market transactions exists. If a legal asset has once been recognized, the subsequent disposal of the legal asset through a market transaction is always recognized.

Rules applying to general changes

B: No general change can be recorded

This rule is explicit enough so that it required little comment. General price level changes, or changes in the pure interest rate have never been recorded. This is in contrast to the fact that specific price level changes in the form of appraisals were at one time recorded by accounting. This is true despite the fact that the evidence for general changes is more objective than the evidence for appraisals.

Rules applicable to specific changes

C: Specific changes evidenced by physical
or legal changes must be recorded

Physical and legal changes are the only specific changes that must be recorded for all categories. An alternative rule stating that "specific changes considered virtually irreversible must be recorded" was considered and rejected. Physical or legal changes are generally irreversible, since a contract once expired does not gain new life, and a building destroyed by fire does not rise from the ashes. All changes demanded by Rule C would thus also be demanded by the alternative rule. However, accounting records "irreversible" economic changes if they affect one category and does not record these events if they affect a different category. Therefore, the rule is restricted to legal and specific changes.

Rules applicable to forecast changes

D-1: Relative changes in forecasts about the life span of existing assets or equities must be recorded, if the original forecase about the life span is supportable by objective and verifiable evidence

D-2: Absolute changes in forecast about assets, not dealing with the life span of the asset, may not be recorded

D-3: An absolute change in forecasts about the life span of an asset may be recorded but only through revision of previously recorded forecasts

Rule D-1 deals with relative changes. Interest charges, interest income, and amortizations all represent relative forecast changes about the life span of an asset or equity. The original forecast about the life of the asset or equity is in each case supported by objective evidence. In the case of interest charges and income, the asset or equity itself specifies when payments are to be received or paid and determines the probable life span. In the case of most physical and legal assets, statistical or legal evidence exist concerning the expected life. Accrual accounting, almost without exception, records interest income and expense accruals and the amortization of physical and legal assets. In areas where the original forecast about life span is more ambiguous (good will, organization costs, and the like), diversity of practice exists. This diversity of practice is permissible under Rule D-1 in the absence of objective evidence about the life span.

Both Rules D-2 and D-3 concern absolute changes in forecasts about assets. First they rule out any recording of forecasts except through revision of previously recorded events, and secondly they rule out revision of previously recorded events unless such revisions are due to a changed forecast about the life span of the asset.

Changed forecasts about service potential or an asset may arise in two ways: either because an asset is expected to have a longer or shorter life than originally envisioned, or because the service remaining in an unchanged span of service life is expected to be smaller or larger than originally anticipated.

The first represents a change in life estimate, the second does not. Both these changes can be consistent with the original cost restraint. The original cost restraint essentially says that the total cost of the service that an asset provides over the entire length of asset life, shal for accounting purposes, be considered a constant -- equal to the asset's original cost. An illustration is in order. An asset was originally acquired five years ago and was expected to last ten years. Two types of absolute forecast changes may now occur.

1. The asset is now not expected to last five more years, but is instead expected to last two more years. This absolute change in the forecast can and may be recorded, through a revision of the previously recorded amortization without violating the original cost restraint. Since fully depreciated assets still in use are sometimes found on balance sheets, it is clear that such revisions need not be recorded. If revisions of life estimate had to be recorded it would be impossible to have fully depreciated assets on hand.
2. A different change in forecasts is as follows: The asset is still expected to last for five more years, but the service attributable to the asset in its remaining life will be smaller (or larger) than originally anticipated. This change also could be recorded through

revising the previously recorded amortization without breeching the original cost restraint. However, this change, not being about the life span, is prohibited by Rule D-2. Thus, the rules in fact provide a stronger restraint than "original cost."

Evidence justifying the existence of these rules is ample. Total obsolescence, i.e., obsolescence shortening the service life of an asset may be recognized (note Rule D-3 permits but does not require such recogniztion). Partial obsolescence whiic implies reduced service but not reduced service life is not recognized.[1]

Support is also found in the following statement:

> It is generally recognized, however, that where circumstances . . . render a particular patent economically ineffective, <u>the process of amortization</u> should be accelerated.[2]

In other words, this economic ineffectiveness is perceived only in terms of a decreased number of periods of service and an acceleration of the amortization process. It is conceivable that "economic ineffectiveness" may represent something other than a reduced life span. If it is recorded, however, it must be recorded in terms of decreased service life.

Rules applicable to conversions

There are no class rules applicable to conversions.

Conclusion

One rule applicable to all events, and seven rules applicable to the various classes were defined in this chapter and are listed in Table 2. Of these rules two (Rules X and D-3) are permissive but not mandatory. They

---

[1] See David Green, Jr. and George H. Sorter, "Accounting for Obsolescense -- A Proposal," Accounting Review, XXXIV, No. 3 (July, 1959), 433-41.

[2] Wixon, p. 19.10. Emphasis supplied.

indicate that an event may be recorded but need not. Four rules (A-1; A-2; C and D-1) are mandatory and positive. These rules insist that certain events be recorded. Rules B and D-2 are mandatory and negative, insisting that certain events not be recorded.

TABLE 2

THE CLASS RULES

Applicable to	Title	Rule
All	X	An event whose recognition is required or sanctioned by a governmental agency may be recorded.
Class A	A-1	All market transactions involving physical assets must be recorded.
	A-2	All market transactions decreasing legal assets must be recorded.
Class B	B	No general change can be recorded.
Class C	C	Specific changes evidenced by physical or legal changes must be recorded.
Class D	D-1	Relative changes in forecasts about the life span of existing assets or equities must be recorded, if the original forecast about the life span is supportable by objective and verifiable evidence.
	D-2	Absolute changes in forecast about assets, not dealing with the life span of the asset may not be recorded.
	D-3	An absolute change in forecasts about the life span of an asset may be recorded but only through revision of previously recorded forecasts.
Class E		None

CHAPTER V

THE CATEGORY RULES

The selection rules that apply to only one category of a given class or classes are listed as Category Rules. These category rules have relevance only for the category to which they apply. Ten category rules are discussed in this chapter. Three rules apply to Category I; one rule applies to Category II; foru rules govern selection for Category III; and two rules are relevant for Category IV.

Rules applicable to Category I -- asset increase / equity increase

Rule I-1: An increase of an asset and the residual responsibility is recorded only if an appropriate quantification of the value of the asset is contained within the asset itself

This rule produces effects somewhat similar to results that would be obtained if the rule had stated that these events are recognized only if a monetary asset is received. The "monetary asset" rule, however, is not appropriate for several reasons. First, there is a general confusion about "monetary" and "moneyness." Second, accounting sometimes does not recognize an event of this category even if the incoming asset is a monetary asset such as a long term note or bond. For instance, income (residual equity increase) is sometimes not recognized when an installment sale is made. In this case the incoming asset -- the installment note -- is clearly a monetary one, but there _might_ be a doubt as to whether the value of the asset is established by looking at the asset alone. How that doubt is resolved would determine whether or not profit is recognized.

Gilman claimed that "claim to cash" is the appropriate distinction for these situations. He states: "the test of realization (i.e., an asset -- residual equity increase) -- therefore demands an actual immediate or deferred effect upon cash, the time lag involved in any deferrent being no element of the test."[1] The fallacy of the "claim to cash" distinction is explained by Vatter: ". . . The note is not a 'claim to cash' at all but a claim against a person who may or may not control an asset fund of sufficient size or liquidity to pay the note now or when it matures."[2] In addition, if the "effect on cash" is in fact deferred, the deferral may affect the recognition of the event. This is the case encountered with installment stales. It is also hard to see why the monetary asset -- real asset distinction and the "claim to cash" criteria should be important to accountants. For instance the value of a share of General Motors stock may be more objectively determinable than the value of Mr. X's note. Mr. X's note, however, can be quantified by looking at the note. Market quotations, appraisals and the like are necessary to quantify real assets. The figures on Mr. X's note remain the same over the life span of the note. An auditor can look at the note at any time and establish the note's life. The market quotation for the stock is appropriate only for that day, and does not suggest an appropriate quantification for the stock as of a preceding or subsequent date.

The rule as stated has clear audit implications. If an appropriate quantification of the value of the asset is part of the asset itself, the quantification of the asset can be verified by merely looking at the asset at any

---

[1] Stephen Gilman, Accounting Concepts of Profit (New York: The Ronald Press Company, 1939), p. 104.

[2] Vatter, p. 30

time. Although the proper number to describe the asset may vary over the asset's life, the appropriate number, or series of numbers, can be identified by looking at the asset at any time.

The main effect of this rule is to prohibit the recognition of income (a residual equity increase) in barter transactions. Since these transactions are rare, evidence to support the rule is also rare. Support for the rule is found in a recently described barter transaction and in the accounting treatment for donations.

One recent barter transaction concerned an advertising agency. This agency wrote and recorded jingles for a radio station in exchange for air time. The air time was later sold to the agency clients. The accounting method adopted was a cost recovery method. The cost of the jingles was reduced by the amount of cash received when the air time was sold. Only after all the cost of the jingles was recorded was income recognized. In this situation, the sale of jingles for air time was recognized as an accounting event only in terms of an exchange of "jingle" for "air time" and not as a revenue producing event.[1]

The rule is consistent with present accounting practices regarding donations and grants. To be consistent, only cash donations, and no other grants or donations, would be recognized as an asset / residual equity increase. This is actually the practice. Cash subsidies for the air lines were included as revenue.[2] Grants or donations of other types of assets are either not recorded -- as in the case for most franchises -- or are recorded as asset / specific equity increases. The specific equity is ususally called donated capital. This is awkward, since generally it is hard to conceive of specific responsibilities

---

[1] See The Texas Certified Public Accountant, XXXI, No. 3 (November, 1958), 87.

[2] See, for instance, Eastern Airline Annual Report, 1950-1956.

arising from a truly unrestricted donation. Equities related to donations are even considered available for dividends. Marple states: "Legally, however, there are very few limitations on the use of this type of surplus. No specific legal restrictions have been found, but a few states include donations with other types of paid in surplus, and in this way place certain restrictions on its use."[1]

A defense can be made of the conventional practice. The most typical donations that appear in the history of profit making concerns are gifts of land, buidlings and the like, which represent inducements to those firms to locate in a particular municipality or area. The utilization of such assets represents an implied commitment, if not a legal obligation, to operate in the area. Of course, when the location decision is made, such a commitment results. However, if the location decision is made freely (without subsidies or inducement), the advantages of the given location presumably outweigh the disadvantages, and no recognition of the commitment is necessary. But when an inducement is offered, and rational behavior on both sides is assumed (a basic assumption of accounting quantifications), the commitment does imply a quantifiable responsibility. The municipality presumably would not have offered an inducement if the company would have located there without it. The inducement, therefore, was intended to overcome some net disadvantage of the proposed location -- untrained workers, lack of transportation, etc. The responsibility to absorb this postulated disadvantage is what the company yields in return for the "donation." But even though a specific responsibility exists, it is not appropriately described by the phrase "donated capital."

---

[1] Raymond F. Marple, Capital Surplus and Corporate Net Worth (New York: The Ronald Press Company, 1936), p. 134.

Rule I-2: An increase of a nonphysical asset and a specific responsibility may be recorded; it must be recorded, if and only if, separate and independent verification of the responsibility exists

This rule effectively prohibits the recording of certain contracts essentially unperformed by both sides. This does not apply to all contracts of this kind. The rule can best be illustrated by an example involving leases. The case for recognition of leases among the assets and equities of a firm has generally revolved around the basic similarity of the leased and owned properties, and the ensuing inconsistency of recognizing only the "owned" item as an accounting asset.[1] It is possible for the potential asset to be absolutely identical in a number of situations and still find a divergence of accounting practice. For instance, compare the following situations:

Situation 1. -- A 99 year lease contract is signed calling for "X" dollars per year rental.

Situation 2. -- An identical lease is signed except that the contract calls for the lessee to sign a note calling for payment of "X" per year.

Situation 3. -- The same 99 year lease is signed, however, the lessee issues common or preferred stock or perhaps long term bonds in an amount equal to the present value of payments of "X" dollars per year.

Accounting practice recognizes neither the asset nor the contractual responsibility arising from Situation 1. Accountants questioned were in substantial agreement that both Situation 2 and Situation 3 would be recognized by accounting. How do these three events differ? The asset assumed in each case is identical. The difference lies in the responsibilities assumed. In Situations 1 and 2, the responsibilities are substantively identical -- the

---

1 See Gordon Shillinglaw, "Leasing and Financial Statements," The Accounting Review, XXXIII, No. 4 (October, 1958), 581-92.

responsibility in both cases consisting of the promise to pay "X" dollars per year. In all three cases the responsibility remains unperformed and in all three cases the rights of the lessor are transferable. Some have argued that the legal responsibilities or legal rights arising from these events might differ if either or both sides were to default or become bankrupt.[1] But for this argument to have force, two conditions must prevail. First, there must be a significant probability of default. In general, and in the absence of evidence to the contrary, accounting assumes that the most probable future facing the accounting unit is one of continuity of operations, a future in which the accounting unit will honor its commitments. Thus, it is not correct to envision a future that consists of default on obligations and, typically, responsibilities are not quantified by the legal penalties.

Even granting a significant probability of default, it is a moot point whether the obligations of the defaulter would be different in any of these situations. The only substantive difference that seems to obtain in these situtations is that the responsibility existing in Situations 2 and 3 is different from the other one. Notes and stock arise from many kinds oftransactions that are normally recognized. Therefore, the existence of notes payable, accounts payable, and common stock is normally verified through routine auditing procedures. It would be almost impossible to ignore these responsibilities and the transactions from which they arose. It would be hard to offset the asset (the rights under the lease) against the responsibility, because the responsibility has an existence of its own, apart from the asset and indpenedent of it. In the case of simple contracts, the document establishing the asset is also the only evidence of the responsibility and the ignoring of both asset and

---

[1] See Alvin Zizes, "Disclosure of Long-Term Leases," Journal of Accountancy, CXI, No. 2 (February, 1961), 37-47.

responsibility is more possible and feasible. It is speculation to suggest that the above is the actual reason for the rule's existence -- however, the rule does exist, and this seems to be the only explanation for accounting practice in this area. The effect of this rule is to deny accounting existence to all sorts of events besides leases. Purchase commitments, wage agreements, and executive compensation agreements are all events that are excluded from the universe of accounting events.

Rule I-3: Specific changes other than legal or physical changes cannot be recorded

For this catgeory only legal or physical changes are recognized. No economic changes are recorded. Compare this rule with Rule II which is applicable to asset / equity decreases.

Rules applicable to category II -- asset decrease / equity decrease

Rule II: A specific change considered virtually irreversible must be recorded

As already mentioned, this rule is more inclusive than class Rule C. It requires the recording of all physical and legal changes and the recognition of economic changes considered irreversible. Current assets must be written down to market value, presumable because such a price change is considered virtually irreversible in view of the short life span of the asset affected.

The writedown of noncurrent assets to market value is another story. Such declines are recorded only if they are permanent, or result in a total loss of value; a decline in the market value of building and equipment is rarely recognized in accounting.[1] Presumably, due to the longer remaining life,

---

1 Wixon, p. 16.6.

accounting considers value declines of noncurrent physical assets to be reversible.

The accounting position in regard to recording market writedowns of legal assets is similar. "A departure from cost in the accounts is warranted only when a significant and relatively permanent decline in value has taken place."[1]

In the case of intangibles, where market values are generally not obtainable, the accounting position seems to be that complete impairment, being irreversible, must be recognized. Partial impairment might be reversible and therefore generally need not be recorded. The periodic amortization of intangibles is of course permitted, but this represents a forecast change and not the recognition of a specific change resulting in parital impairment.

Support for this view is found in the following:

> If a patent proves to have no value before the expiration of its useful life, a lump sum write off is required.[2]
>
> . . . if its (good will) value is permanently impaired, the loss should be recognized in the accounts.[3]

The fact that the above rule is applicable to asset decreases, but not to asset increases, is part of the operational context of the oft-cited "Principle of Conservatism."

---

1 *Ibid*., p. 13.18. Emphasis supplied.

2 *Ibid*., p. 19.11. Emphasis supplied.

3 *Ibid*., p. 19.18. Emphasis supplied.

Rules applicable to Category III -- asset increase / asset decrease

Rule III-1: If the utilization of an asset is economically beneficial to the production process as a whole, a part of the utilized asset must be converted into each individual physical asset produced.

This rule gives operational context to the "costs-attach" notion, requires "conventional costing" and rejects "direct costing" for financial reports. The impact of the rule is quite plain, although the statement of the rule is cumbersome. If a machine is necessary for the production of gadgets, then as each gadget is produced, part of the cost of the machine is assigned to it -- i.e., part of the machine is converted and must be converted into each gadget produced.

This rule is perfectly consistent with the use of "normal absorption costing" rather than "full absorption costing." Under "normal absorption costing" if production falls below a certain level, only part of the cost of the machine is assigned to each gadget. The rule requires not that all of the machine be converted into all of the gadgets, but rather that some of the machine be converted into all of the gadgets. This requirement is fulfilled by all of the conventional costing methods, but not by "direct" or "relevant costing."[1] Evidence for this rule is found in the position of the AAA[2] and the AICPA[3] in their stand against direct costing.

---

[1] See George H. Sorter and Charles T. Horngren, "Asset Recognition and Economic Attributes -- the Relevant Costing Approach," The Accounting Review, XXXVII, No. 3 (July, 1962), 391-99.

[2] American Accounting Association, p. 4.

[3] American Institute of Certified Public Accountants, Accounting Research Bulletin, No. 43 (New York: American Institute of Certified Public Accountants, 1953), p.29.

Rule III-2: A conversion of an existing asset into a legal asset may be recorded

Assets which expire in the process of developing a patent may be converted into the patent -- i.e., the patent may be quantified by the expired assets.

Rule III-3: A conversion of any existing asset into an economic asset may not be recorded

This rule effectively prohibits the continued existence of any economic asset apart from good will. Why is good will the only intangible economic asset recognized? Other possible intangible economic assets, such as employee morale, customer acceptance, employee skill, and the functioning pattern of managerial organization are not acquired directly. Employee morale might be acquired through expenditures for recreation facilities or washrooms. Customer acceptance can result from advertising expenditures, and employee skills may be developed in training programs. Therefore, these economic assets are not directly acquired. The recognition of consumer acceptance would require the following entries:

(1) Advertising services
Cash

(2) Consumer acceptance
Advertising services

Consumer acceptance is not the advertising campaign for which the expenditure was made but rather the result of that campaign. The conversion of the asset "advertising services" into "consumer acceptance" would be necessary for "consumer acceptance" to be shown as an asset, and it is this conversion that is prohibited.

Rule III-4: A specific change considered virtually irreversible must be recorded

This rule is identical to Category Rule II.

Rule applicable to Category IV -- equity increase / equity decrease

Rule IV-1: Any event of this category that affects the legal nature of specific responsibilities must be recorded

Rule IV-2: A forecast of a likely increase in specific responsibilities must be recorded

This category represents the only area where forecasts concerning something besides the life span of an asset or equity may be recorded.

Without defining "likely" precisely, an event that will probably increase responsibilities may be recorded. Probable and estimated liabilities are often recorded by the accounting process usually under the title of reserves.

Conclusion

The ten rules applicable to the various categories were defined and explained in this chapter. Table 3 illustrates the effect of the rules on the 125 events. The table indicates whether the event exists; and if it exists, whether or not it is recorded. Also indicated are the rules applicable to each event. This table is analyzed in detail in the succeeding chapter.

TABLE 3

THE ACCOUNTING UNIVERSE

Category	Class									
	Market Transactions		General Changes		Specific Changes		Forecast Changes		Conversion	
	A		B		C		D		E	
	Recorded	Rule	Recorded	Rule	Recorded	Rule	Recorded	Rule	Recorded	Rule
I. Asset Increase / Equity Increase										
1. Physical - Residual	+	A-1 I-1	-	B	-	I-3	+	D-3	+	A-1
2. Physical - Specific	+	A-1	-	B	-	I-3	-	I-2	0	
3. Legal - Residual	+	I-1	-	B	-	I-3	+	D-1	0	
4. Legal - Specific	+	I-2	-	B	-	I-3	-	I-2	+	X
5. Economic - Residual	-	I-1	-	B	-	I-3	-	I-1	0	
6. Economic - Specific	+	I-1	-	B	-	I-3	-	I-2	0	
II. Asset Decrease / Equity Decrease										
1. Physical - Residual	+	A-1	-	B	+	II-1	+	D-1 D-3	0	
2. Physical - Specific	+	A-1	-	B	0		0		0	
3. Legal - Residual	+	A-2	-	B	+	II-1	+	D-1 D-3	0	
4. Legal - Specific	+	A-2	-	B	0		0		0	
5. Economic - Residual	0		-	B	+	II-1	+	D-1 D-3	0	
6. Economic - Specific	0		-	B	0		0		0	

III. Asset Increase / Asset Decrease										
1. Physical - Physical	+	A-1	-	B	+	III-4	0		+	III-1
2. Physical - Legal	+	A-1 A-2	-	B	0		0		+	III-1
3. Physical - Economic	+	A-1	-	B	0		0		+	III-1
4. Legal - Physical	+	A-1	-	B	+	III-4	0		+	III-2
5. Legal - Legal	+	A-2	-	B	+	III-4	0		+	III-2
6. Legal - Economic	0		-	B	0		0		+	III-2
7. Economic - Physical	+	A-1	-	B	0		0		-	III-3
8. Economic - Legal	+	A-2	-	B	0		0		-	III-3
9. Economic - Economic	0		-	B	0		0		-	III-3

IV. Equity Increase / Equity Decrease										
1. Specific - Residual	0		-	B	+	C IV-1	+	IV-2 D-1	+	IV-1
2. Specific - Specific	+	IV-1	-	B	0		0		0	
3. Residual - Specific	+	IV-1	-	B	+	C IV-1	0		0	
4. Residual - Residual	0		-	B	0		0		0	

\+ indicated the event is recorded
\- indicated the event is not recorded
0 indicated the event does not exist
The letters and Roman numerals refer to the rule

TABLE 4

THE SELECTION RULES

Applicable to	Title	Rule
All events	X	An event whose recognition is required or sanctioned by a governmental agency may be recorded.
Class A	A-1	All market transactions involving physical assets must be recorded.
	A-2	All market transactions decreasing legal assets must be recorded.
Class B	B	No general change can be recorded.
Class C	C	Specific changes evidenced by physical or legal changes must be recorded.
Class D	D-1	Relative changes in forecasts about the life span of existing assets or equities must be recorded, if the original forecast about the life span is supportable by objective and verifiable evidence.
	D-2	Absolute changes in forecast about assets, not dealing with the life span of the asset may not be recorded.
	D-3	An absolute change in forecasts about the life span of an asset may be recorded but only through revision of previously recorded forecasts.
Category I	I-1	An increase of an asset and the residual responsibility is recorded only if an appropriate quantification of the value of an asset is contained within the asset itself.
	I-2	An increase of a nonphysical asset and a specific responsibility may be recorded; it must be recorded, if and only if, separate and independent verification of the responsibility exists.
	I-3	Specific changes other than legal or physical changes cannot be recorded.
Category II	II	A specific change considered virtually irreversible must be recorded.
Category III	III-1	If the utilization of an asset is economically beneficial to the production process as a whole, a part of the utilized asset must be converted into each individual physical asset produced.
	III-2	A conversion of an existing asset into a legal asset may be recorded.
	III-3	A conversion of any existing asset into an economic asset may not be recorded
	III-4	A specific change considered virtually irreversible must be recorded.
Category IV	IV-1	Any event of this category that affects the legal nature of specific responsibilities must be recorded.
	IV-2	A forecast of a probable increase in specific responsibilities must be recorded.

CHAPTER VI

THE ANALYSIS OF ACCOUNTING EVENTS

The organizational framework developed in chapter ii yields one hundred and twenty-five types of events. In this chapter each one of these events is examined to see whether or not accounting recognition of the event is governed by the rules proposed in chapters iv and v. For each event or group of events the following is provided:

(1) An example

(2) The possible accounting entry

(3) The accounting treatment (i.e., whether the event is recognized or not)

(4) The applicable rule

(5) A comment when needed on the effect of the rules

In order to facilitate the exposition, a table summarizing the accounting treatment is presented preceding the analysis of each category of events. This chapter serves two purposes: (1) it provides a test of the rules that are proposed, (2) it makes it possible to look at any given event and find the accounting treatment as well as the rules for the event.

TABLE 6

ACCOUNTING UNIVERSE--CATEGORY I. ASSET INCREASE / EQUITY INCREASE

Category	Class									
	Market Transactions		General Changes		Specific Changes		Forecast Changes		Conversion	
	A		B		C		D		E	
	Recorded	Rule	Recorded	Rule	Recorded	Rule	Recorded	Rule	Recorded	Rule
1. Physical - Residual	+	A-1 I-1	-	B	-	I-3	+	D-3	+	A-1
2. Physical - Specific	+	A-1	-	B	-	I-3	-	I-2	0	
3. Legal - Residual	+	I-1	-	B	-	I-3	+	D-1	0	
4. Legal- Specific	+	I-2	-	B	-	I-3	-	I-2	+	X
5. Economic - Residual	-	I-1	-	B	-	I-3	-	I-1	0	
6. Economic - Specific	+	I-1	-	B	-	I-3	-	I-2	0	

+ indicates the event is recorded
- indicates the event is not recorded
0 indicates the event does not exist
The letters and Roman numerals refer to the rules governing recognition.

Category I

Type I-A (1) Market transaction resulting in a physical asset / residual equity increase

Example 1: The inflow part of a cash sales transaction

Entry. -- Dr. Cash
Cr. Sales (Residual equity)

Accounting treatment. -- The event is recognized.

Applicable rules: A-1; I-1. -- All exchanges in which the inflowing asset can be quantified independent of the outflow are treated as the sum of two separate and distinct events -- an inflow and an outflow. Rule A-1 demands the recording of a cash sale. Since the incoming asset -- cash -- clearly satisfies Rule I-1, a cash sale is recorded as the sum of an inflow and an outflow. The inflow is an event of this type and is recorded as shown above.

Example 2: The inflow part of a barter sales tramsaction

Entry. -- Dr. Inventory
or Plant
Cr. Sales (residual equity)

Accounting treatment. -- The event is recognized only as an exchange and not as a distinct inflow and outflow.

Applicable rules: A-1; I-1. -- Rule A-1 demands the recognition of a barter transaction. But the incoming asset in this case does not qualify under Rule I-1, and therefore a barter transaction is not recognized as a sum of an inflow and an outflow. The transaction is recognized as an exchange, i.e., an Asset Increase / Asset Decrease type of event not affecting the residual equity. The transaction is recorded as Category III event, and not as a combination Category I and Category II event.

Example 3: Donations of cash

<u>Entry</u>. -- Dr. Cash
Cr. Residual Equity

<u>Accounting treatment</u>. -- The event is recognized.

<u>Applicable rules: A-1; I-1</u>. -- Rule A-1 demands the recognition of inflows or physical assets, and since cash fulfills the requirements of Rule I-1 the donation of cash is recognized as an event of this type.

Example 4: Donations of physical assets other than cash

<u>Entry</u>. -- Dr. Plant
Cr. Residual Equity

<u>Accounting treatment</u>. -- The event is recognized but as an event of the I-A(2) type rather than of the I-1(1) type.

<u>Applicable rules: A-1; I-1</u>. -- Rule A-1 demands the recognition of donations of physical assets. Rule I-1 prohibits the recognition of this event as an event increasing the residual equity. The solution lies in treating the event an an increase of the specific equity -- donated capital -- rather than as an increase of the residual equity.

<u>Type I-A (2) Market transaction resulting in a physical asset / specific equity increase</u>

Example 1: The issue of common stock or debentures

<u>Entry</u>. -- Dr. Cash
Cr. Contributed Capital or Bonds Payable

<u>Accounting treatment</u>. -- The event is recorded.

<u>Applicable rule: A-1</u>.

Example 2: Credit purchases of inventory or other physical assets

<u>Entry</u>. -- Dr. Inventory
Cr. Accounts Payable

<u>Accounting treatment</u>. -- The event is recognized.

<u>Applicable rule: A-1</u>. -- Rule A-1 clearly requires the recording of the above events.

Example 3: Donations of physical assets other than cash

<u>Entry</u>. -- Dr. Land
or Plant
Cr. Donated Capital

<u>Accounting treatment</u>. -- The event is recorded.

<u>Applicable rule: A-1</u>. -- Rule A-1 demands the recognition of donations of physical asset. Rule I-1 prohibits the recognition of this event as an event increasing the residual equity. The solution lies in treating the event as an increase of the specific equity -- donated capital -- rather than as an increase of the residual equity.

<u>Type I-A (3) Market transaction resulting in a legal asset / residual equity increase</u>

Example 1: The inflow part of a credit sales transaction

<u>Entry</u>. -- Dr. Accounts Receivable
Cr. Sales (Residual Equity)

<u>Accounting treatment</u>. -- The event is recorded.

<u>Applicable rules: A-1; I-1</u>. -- All exchanges in which the inflowing asset can be quantified independent of the outflow, are treated as the sum of two separate and distinct events -- an inflow and an outflow. Rule A-1 demands the recording of a credit sale. Since the incoming asset -- accounts receivable --

satisfied Rule I-1, a credit sale is recorded as the sum of an inflow and an outflow. The inflow is an event of this type and is recorded as shown above.

Example 2: The inflow part of an
installment sales transaction

Entry. -- Dr. Installment Notes Receivable
Cr. Sales (Residual Equity)

Accounting treatment. -- The transaction may be recognized as an event of this type or as an exchange and a specific responsibility increase.

Applicable rules: A-1; I-1. -- Rule A-1 demands that installment sales be recognized. If the incoming asset -- the installment note -- is considered to meet the requirements of Rule I-1, the inflow is recognized as an event of this type. If the value of the instalment note is not thought to be contained within the asset, the installment sale is described by the following entries:

(a) Dr. Installment Note
Cr. Inventory

(b) Dr. Installment Note
Dr. Deferred Profit

In that case the installment sale is a combination of an exchange and an asset / specific equity increase rather than a combination of an asset / residual equity increase and an asset / residual equity decrease. It is hard to conceive what the specific responsibility created might be but both methods are found in practice.

Type I-A (4) Market transaction resulting in
a legal asset / specific equity increase

Example 1: The signing of a lease,
wage, or purchase contract

Entry. -- Dr. Leases
or Wage Contract
or Purchase Contract
Cr. Contract Obligations

Accounting treatment. -- The event is not recorded.

Applicable rule: I-2. -- The responsibility in these cases cannot be independently verified and Rule I-2 prohibits the recognition of these events. The contract serves as evidence for both asset and equity. Contractual obligations usually exist concurrently with contractual rights and both obligations and rights can easily be quantified by identical amounts. This makes offset and mutual nonrecognition easy. Contrast that with the obligations under a note payable. A note payable may have been given for any number of possible services -- many of which may have expired or may exist long after the note has been paid. An offsetting asset may not exist and therefore notes payable need to be audited. In the example provided in chapter v, the note payable given for the lease is audited with all other notes payable, and therefore has an independent and auditable existence apart from any possible offsetting asset. The real substantive question that emerges is whether the possibility of offset should affect the recording of events?

Example 2: The acquisition of patents on credit

Entry. -- Dr. Patents
Cr. Notes Payable
or Accounts Payable

Accounting treatment. -- The event is recorded.

Applicable rule: I-2. -- The above equities fulfil the conditions of Rule I-2 and the event is recorded.

Example 3: The acquisition of various services such as labor, advertising, etc. on account

Entry. -- Dr. Services
Cr. Wages Payable
or Miscellaneous Payable

Accounting treatment. -- The event is recorded.

Applicable rule: I-2. -- This event can be recognized under Rule I-2 because wages payable or miscellaneous payables are independently verifiable. However, the signing of a contract for services is not recorded.

Type I-A (5) Market transaction resulting in an economic asset / residual equity increase

Example: The inflow part of a donation to charity

Entry. -- Dr. Good will (?)
Cr. Sales (Residual Equity)

Accounting treatment. -- The event, if it exists, is not recorded as an event of this type. Donations are recorded as Category II events.

Applicable rule: I-1. -- It is hard to conceive os such an event. Perhaps the donation of inventory to a charity could be recorded as:

(a) Dr. Good will
Cr. Sales

and (b) Dr. Cost of Goods Sold
Cr. Inventory

Luckily we do not have to strain our imagination too hard since the recording of the event is clearly prohibited by Rule I-1.

Type I-A (6) Market transaction resulting in an economic asset / specific equity increase

Example: Purchase of good will through issue of stock

Entry. -- Dr. Good will
Dr. Contributed Capital

Accounting treatment. -- The event is recorded.

Applicable rule: I-2. -- Since the responsibility can be verified independently, the event is recorded. It is never recorded by itself, but always as part of a more complex transaction such as the admissions of partners or the purchase of a business concern.

Type I-B (1, 2, 3, 4, 5, 6) A general change resulting in any asset / equity increase

Example: A write-up of an asset reflecting a change in a general price index or in the basic rate of interest

Entry. -- Dr. Any Asset
Cr. Any Responsibility

Accounting treatment. -- These events are not recorded.

Applicable rule: B. -- Rule B prohibits the recording of general changes.

Type I-C (1, 2) A specific change resulting in a physical asset / equity increase

Example 1: An appraisal of plant

Entry. -- Dr. Plant
Cr. Residual Equity or "Appraisal Surplus"

Accounting treatment. -- The event is not recognized.

Applicable rule: I-3.

Example 2: A write-up of an existing physical asset to market

Entry. -- Dr. Inventory
Cr. Residual Equity

Accounting treatment. -- The event is not recognized.

Applicable rule: I-3.

Example 3: The recording of a change in a specific price index

Entry. -- Dr. Machine
Cr. Residual Equity or "Capital Surplus"

Accounting treatment. -- The event is not recognized.

Applicable rule: I-3.

Example 4: Accretion -- the growth of timber and/or other crops

Entry. -- Dr. Crop, timber
Cr. Residual Equity
or "Capital Surplus"

Accounting treatment. -- The event is not recognized except indirectly.

Applicable rules: I-3; X. -- These events are precluded from accounting recognition by Rule I-3. All the available evidence indicates that these events are not recognized in practice, despite the fact that many prominent accounting writers have argued fro the recognition of accretion.[1] The Accounting Handbook states:

> Periodic recognition of accretion has not been widely adopted in practice.[2]

Rowbury finds that:

> Many leading accountants agree that accretion should logically be entered on the books, but no one has set up a system for doing this.[3]

The annual reports of timber companies reveal that accretion has not been recognized.[4] Sometimes accretion is recognized indirectly by valuing ending inventory at market. This occurs only when no cost figures are readily available, and when this inventory valuation is permitted by the Internal Revenue Service. Under these circumstances, it is not accretion but the existence of the ending inventory that is recognized. Such recognition, sanctioned by a governmental agency is allowed by Rule X. The attitude of accounting toward this indirect recognition of accretion is reflected by the following quotations:

---

[1] William A. Paton and William A. Paton, Jr., Asset Accounting (New York: The Macmillan Company, 1952), p. 458.

[2] Wixon, p. 5.6.

[3] James Rowbury, Jr., "Timber Depletion," Accounting Review, XXII, No. 2, (April, 1947), 188-89.

[4] See, for instance, annual reports 1954-1960 of United States Plywood Corporation and Weyerhaeuser Timber Co.

> The use of adjusted selling price in this connection is a <u>convenient</u> solution.[1]

> Where accurate costs have been kept, the cost basis of inventory is preferable, but in case this method cannot be used, it is advisable to deduct a certain amount, say 10%, from the value determined by the market price method.[2]

Example 5: The increase of livestock

<u>Entry</u>. -- Dr. Livestock
Cr. Residual Equity

<u>Accounting treatment</u>. -- The event is not recognized as one of this type.

<u>Applicable rules: C; I-3</u>. -- It might appear that a conflict exists between class Rule C and Category Rule I-3. The increase of livestock certainly represents a change in the physical form of an asset, and thus should be recorded under Rule C. An event may be described merely through a change in names, i.e., treated as an asset exchange. The increase can be (and often is) described as follows:

Dr. Livestock
Cr. Brood Stock

This is similar to the recognition of a rights declaration affecting investments owned. There the change in the legal nature of the asset is described as an exchange, i.e.,

Dr. Rights
Cr. Investment in Stock

Example 6: The discovery of new or additional mineral deposits

<u>Entry</u>. -- Dr. Mineral Deposits
Cr. Residual Equity
or "Discovery Surplus"

---

[1] Carl Devine, <u>Inventory Valuation and Periodic Income</u> (New York: Ronald Press Company, 1942), p. 155.

[2] C.W. Collings, "Ranch Accounting," in Roy B. Kester, <u>Accounting Theory and Practice</u> (New York: Ronald Press Company, 1921), p. 243.

Accounting treatment. -- The event is not recognized.

Applicable rule: I-3. -- This event is not recorded by the accounting process, to the dismay of certain accounting theorists. Paton and Paton remark:

> Here is a point where conventional accounting which generally fails to recognize such increases in property systematically is especially weak.[1]
>
> There is no more sense in omitting from the accounting records the value of demonstrated increases in the amount of coal, copper, or petroleum, natural gas and so on, than there would be in neglecting to record assets received through the process of inheritance.[2]

Type I-C (3) A specific change resulting in a legal asset / residual equity increase

Example: The write-up of marketable securities to market

Entry. -- Dr. Securities
Cr. Residual Equity

Accounting treatment. -- The event is not recognized.

Applicable Rule: I-3. -- Rule I-3 prohibits the recognition of this event.

Type I-c (4) A specific change resulting in a legal asset / specific equity increase

Example: The write-up of marketable securities to market

Entry. -- Dr. Securities
Cr. Unrealized Market Gain

Accounting treatment. -- The event is recognized only when recognition is sanctioned by a governmental agency.

Applicable rules: X; I-3. -- The SEC requires marketable securities of regulated investment companies to be carried at market values.[3] For these

---

1 Paton and Paton, p. 450.

2 Ibid.

3 United States Securities and Exchange Commission, "Accounting Series Release #57," Accounting Series Releases (Washington: U.S. Government Printing Office, 1948), p. 173.

companies Rule X permits the recording of this type of event. For all other companies Rule I-3 prohibits the recognition of the value change.

<u>Type I-C (5, 6) A specific change resulting in an economic asset / equity increase</u>

Example: The recognition of the increased value of good will

<u>Entry</u>. -- Dr. Good will
Cr. Residual Equity
or Unrealized Appreciation

<u>Accounting treatment</u>. -- The event is not recognized.

<u>Applicable rule: I-3</u>.

<u>Type I-D (1, 3, 5) A forecast resulting in an asset / residual equity increase</u>

Example 1: The earning of "interest income"

<u>Entry</u>. -- Dr. Investment
or Interest Receivable
Cr. Interest Income (Residual Equity)

<u>Accounting treatment</u>. -- The event is recorded.

<u>Applicable rule: D-1</u>. -- The earning of interest income as disucssed in chapter iii is a relative forecast change. The forecast about the life span of the asset is specified by the terms of the investment acquired and is therefore objective and verifiable. The subsequent earning of interest describes the effect of time upon this change in the forecast about the money to be received and is recognized under Rule D-1.

Example 2: The recognition of income by the "percentage of completion" basis

<u>Entry</u>. -- Dr. Accounts Receivable
or Unbilled Charges
Cr. Revenue (Residual Equity)

<u>Accounting treatment</u>. -- The event is recognized in some cases.

Applicable rule: D-1. -- When production of a special order is undertaken under contract, profit may be recognized as production proceeds.

Because of Rule I-2, no entry is made at the time the contract is negotiated. This nonrecognition can be thought of as due to offsetting the results of the following entry:

(1) Dr. Accounts Receivable
Cr. Forecast Offset

This forecast offset measures the life span of the receivable. The receivable will be collected when the construction has been completed. In this case, the life span of the receivable is measured by stages of construction rather than units of time, just as the life span of a wasting asset is expressed in units of product instead of units of time. As production proceeds, there is a relative forecast change indicating that collection is more imminent and that the life span of the receivable has been shortened. Had entry (1) been recorded, this forecast change would be recorded by the following entry:

(2) Dr. Forecast Offset
Cr. Revenue (Residual Equity)

Combining entries (1) and (2) results in the entry (3) used in recording income under the "percentage of completion" method.

(3) Dr. Accounts Receivable
Cr. Revenue

The forecast offset can also be thought of as a specific responsibility for unperformed service, in which case the revenue represents the reduction of the responsibility and income would be recognized in an identical fashion.

Example 3: The revision of previously recorded depreciation

Entry. -- Dr. Accumulated Depreciation
Cr. Residual Equity

Accounting treatment. -- The event may be recognized.

Applicable rule: D-3. -- If the proposed revision of the depreciation is due to a change in the life estimate of the asset, the event may be recognized under Rule D-3.

Type I-D (2, 4, 6) A forecast resulting in an asset / specific equity increase

These events do not exist.

Type I-E (1) A conversion resulting in a physical asset / residual equity increase

Example: The mining of gold

Entry. -- Dr. Gold
Cr. Revenue (Residual Equity)

Accounting treatment. -- The event is recognized.

Applicable Rule: I-1. -- The refining of gold represents the only conversion where a reasonable quantification of the assets' value is contained within the asset and the only conversion activity recognizable under Rule I-1.

Type I-E (2) A conversion resulting in a physical asset / specific equity increase

Example: Capitalization of interest during construction

Entry. -- Dr. Plant
Cr. Interest Payable

Accounting treatment. -- The event is recognized by regulated industries.

Applicable Rule: X. -- The capitalization of interest by regulated industries during construction is sanctioned by regulatory agencies and comes within the scope of Rule X. Nonregulated industries generally do not recognize this event.

Type I-E (3, 4, 5, 6) A conversion resulting in a legal or economic asset / equity

These events do not exist.

TABLE 6

ACCOUNTING UNIVERSE--CATEGORY II. ASSET DECREASE / EQUITY DECREASE

Category	Class									
	Market Transactions		General Changes		Specific Changes		Forecast Changes		Conversion	
	A		B		C		D		E	
	Recorded	Rule	Recorded	Rule	Recorded	Rule	Recorded	Rule	Recorded	Rule
1. Physical - Residual	+	A-1	-	B	+	II-1	+	D-1 D-3	0	
2. Physical - Specific	+	A-1	-	B	0		0		0	
3. Legal - Residual	+	A-2	-	B	+	II-1	+	D-1 D-3	0	
4. Legal - Specific	+	A-2	-	B	0		0		0	
5. Economic - Residual	0		-	B	+	II-1	+	D-1 D-3	0	
6. Economic - Specific	0		-	B	0		0		0	

+ indicates the event is recorded
- indicates the event is not recorded
0 indicates the event does not exist
The letters and Roman numerals refer to the rules governing recognition.

Category II

Type II-A (1) Market transaction resulting in a physical asset / residual equity decrease

Example 1: The outflow protion of a sales transaction

Entry. -- Dr. Cost of Goods Sold (Residual E uity)
Cr. Inventory

Accounting treatment. -- The event is recognized if the inflow portion of the sales transaction meets the test of Rule I-1.

Applicable rule: A-1. -- An asset exchange is treated as a combination inflow-outflow event if the incoming asset qualifies under Rule I-1. If not, the exchange is treated as a single Category III event.

Example 2: The disposition of a noncurrent asset

Entry. -- Dr. Accumulated Depreciation
Dr. Residual Equity
Cr. Plant & Equipment

Accounting treatment. -- The event is recognized.

Applicable rule: A-1. -- The disposition of noncurrent assets is usually recorded through a compound entry, also recording the proceeds resulting from the disposition. The entry would be:

Dr. Accumulated Depreciation
Dr. Cash
Dr. or Credit Residual Equity
Cr. Plant & Equipment

This entry combines the recording of the inflow (a Category I event) and the outflow (a Category II event). This is possible whenever the new asset received qualifies under Rule I-1. In the case of trade-ins where the new asset does not meet the test of Rule I-1, the usual practice is not to record any gains or losses. Instead, the trade-in is recognized as an exchange by the following entry:

Dr. Accumulated Depreciation - Old Asset
Dr. New Asset
Cr. Old Asset
Cr. Cash

Example 3: The incurrence of expense by cash payments

The reasons for not considering this occurrence as an event of this type has already been discussed.[1]

Type II-A (2) Market transaction resulting in a physical asset / specific equity decrease

Example: The discharge of specific responsibilities such as the repayment of debts or retirement of bonds or stock

Entry. -- Dr. Accounts Payable
or Contributed Capital
Cr. Cash

Accounting treatment. -- The event is recognized.

Applicable rule: A-1.

Type II-A (3) Market transaction resulting in a legal asset / residual equity decrease

Example: The outflow part of a sale of a legal asset

Entry. -- Dr. Residual Equity
Cr. Investment
or Patent

Accounting treatment. -- The event is recognized but usually the inflow and outflow would be recorded in one entry.

Applicable rule: A-2. -- See comment for Type II-A-1, example 3.

---

[1] See chapter iii, above.

<u>Type II-A (4) Market transaction resulting in a legal asset / specific equity decrease</u>

Example: The collection of factored accounts

<u>Entry</u>. -- Dr. Due to Factor
Cr. Accounts Receivable

<u>Accounting treatment</u>.-- The event is recognized.

<u>Applicable rule: A-2</u>.

<u>Type II-A (5, 6) Market transaction resulting in an economic asset / equity decrease</u>

An unlikely event.

<u>Type II-B (1, 2, 3, 4, 5, 6) A general change resulting in an asset / equity decrease</u>

Example: The write down of an asset reflecting a change in a general price index or in the basic rate of interest

<u>Entry</u>. -- Dr. Any Responsibility
Cr. Any Asset

<u>Accounting treatment</u>. -- These events are not recorded.

<u>Applicable rule: B</u>. -- Rule B forbids the recognition of all general changes.

<u>Type II-C (1, 3, 5) A specific change resulting in an asset / residual equity decrease</u>

Example 1: The full or partial loss of an asset due to fire or theft

<u>Entry</u>. -- Dr. Loss (Residual Equity)
Cr. Building
or Inventory, etc.

<u>Accounting treatment</u>. -- The event is recorded.

Applicable rule: II-1. -- The recognition of this type of event is required by Rule II-1, as well as by Rule C.

Example 2: The write-down of a current asset to market

Entry. -- Dr. Residual Equity
Cr. Inventory
or Short Term Investments

Accounting treatment. -- The event is recorded.

Applicable rule: II-1. -- The recognition of this type of event is required by Rule II-1. The asset is current and will be utilized in the short-run future, and a market decline is therefore considered irreversible. The existence of Rule II-1 and the lack of a similar rule for Category I is one of the manifestations of the "principle of conservatism."

Example 3: The write-down of a noncurrent asset to market or appraised value

Entry. -- Dr. Residual Equity
Cr. Plant
or Accumulated Depreciation

Accounting treatment. -- This event is usually recorded only if the market value falls to zero.

Applicable rule: II-1. -- This type of write-down is seldom encountered, except when the asset has lost all value. The greater remaining life of noncurrent assets makes a reversal of value changes more probably than for current assets. If the value falls to zero, this value change is definite, easier to quantify by a single number, and unlikely to be reversed.

Example 4: The expiration of services that had been acquired

Entry. -- Dr. Expense (Residual Equity)
or Loss
Cr. Services

<u>Accounting treatment</u>. -- These events are recognized if no prior conversion has been recorded.

<u>Applicable rule: II-1</u>. -- The acquisitions of all services -- advertising, legal, labor, etc. -- result in an acquisition of an asset. The acquired asset is a legal asset, representing the right to the services to be performed. When a worker reports fro work, or a lawyer lifts the receiver of his phone, or an accountant sharpens his pencil, all in exchange for valuable consideration, the accounting unit acquires the right to the man's time and effort. As the worker works or loafs, as the lawyer talks and as the accountant figures -- the services are performed, and the right to the services terminated. If there are any rights, they apply to the benefits resulting from the services. If there is no future benefit, and no conversion to another asset has therefore been recorded, the expiration of the service must be recorded under Rule II-1. The expiration of the rights to the services will have been recorded either implicitly through a conversion to another asset or explicitly through an event of this type.

Example 5: The write-off of an uncollectible
account if an allowance system is not used

<u>Entry</u>. -- Dr. Residual Equity
Cr. Accounts Receivable

<u>Accounting treatment</u>. -- The event is recorded.

<u>Applicable rule: II-1</u>. -- If an allowance system of recording uncollectibility is not used, the probable nonpayment of a debt is recorded as above. If an allowance system is used the actual write-off is recorded by the following entry:

Dr. Estimated Uncollectible Accounts
Cr. Accounts Receivable

which represents an asset increase / asset decrease type of event. This is an appropriate place to discuss the original estimate of uncollectibility if an allowance system is used. This estimate is usually recorded as follows:

Dr. "Bad Debt Expense" (Residual Equity)
Cr. Estimated Uncollectible Accounts

and would appear to be an asset / equity decrease event, resulting from a forecast. The above entry suggests that "bad debts" represent an additional outflow. However, the cost of the goods delivered to the customer is already included in the cost of goods account whether the customer pays or not. By considering "bad debts" as an expense, two expenses in connection with bad debts are recorded -- the cost of the goods given away, and the nonpayment for these goods. The more logical treatment is to consider the uncollectibility as a non-inflow. In effect, two prices are charged for the goods delivered. For those customers (X) who will pay, the price is, say $1.00; for those customers (Y) who will not pay, the price is zero. The sales revenue is not "X + Y" times $1.00, but rather X(1.00) and Y(0.00). The second term drops out and the revenue should be recognized as X(1.00). This is the result obtained by treating the estimated uncollectibility as a revenue deduction.

<u>Type II-C (2, 4, 6) A specific change resulting in an asset / specific equity decrease</u>

Specific changes cannot decrease an asset and a specific responsibility and these events do not exist.

<u>Type II-D (1, 3, 5) A forecast resulting in an asset / specific residual equity decrease</u>

Example 1: The recognition of depreciation or depletion

<u>Entry</u>. -- Dr. Expense (Residual Equity)
Cr. Accumulated Depreciation or Accumulated Depletion

<u>Accounting treatment</u>. -- The event is recognized if no prior conversion has been recorded.

Applicable rule: D-1. -- Depreciation and depletion are relative forecast changes about the life span of an asset. For most depreciation methods, the life span is considered a function of time; in the case of "use" depreciation and depletion, the life span is expressed in terms of units of use. In any case, these events are recorded under Rule D-1, if no prior conversion has been recorded. The service rendered by the asset may result in increased service potential of another asset and such a conversion may have been recorded. The forecast about the decreased life span thus may be recorded implicitly through a conversion entry, or explicitly through the above entry.

Example 2: Revision of previously
recorded depreciation

Entry. -- Dr. Residual Equity
Cr. Accumulated Depreciation

Accounting treatment. -- The event may be recognized.

Applicable rule: D-2; D-3. -- If the revision is due to a changed estimate of service life, it may be recorded under Rule D-3. All other forecast changes cannot be recorded.

Example 3: Amortization of patents,
lease holds, etc.

Entry. -- Dr. Expense (Residual Equity)
Cr. Patent, etc.

Accounting treatment. -- The event is recorded.

Applicable rule: D-1. -- Objective verifiable evidence as to the legal (if not economic) life of the above assets exists, and the amortization (a forecast change) is recorded under Rule D-1.

Example 4: Amortization of "Good will"

Entry. -- Dr. Expense (Residual Equity)
Cr. Good will

Accounting treatment. -- The event may be recorded.

Applicable rule: D-1. -- The estimated service life of physical assets is generally supportable by statistical evidence, and the legal life span of legal assets is generally specified, by contract or agreement. The life span of "good will" is open to question and controversy. It is not surprising that a veriety of "amortization" methods ranging from "none" to "all" are employed. This is permitted by Rule D-1.

Type II-D (2, 4, 6) A forecast resulting in an asset / specific equity increase

No such event exists.

Type II-E (1, 2, 3, 4, 5, 6) A conversion resulting in an asset / equity decrease

No conversion resulting in an asset / equity decrease exists.

Category III

Type III-A (1) Market transaction resulting in a physical asset increase / physical asset decrease

Example: The purchase of inventory or equipment

Entry. -- Dr. Inventory
or Plant
Cr. Cash

Accounting treatment. -- The event is recognized.

Applicable rules: A-1; I-1. -- The new asset does not qualify under Rule I-1 and the event must be recognized as an exchange not affecting the residual equity.

TABLE 7

ACCOUNTING UNIVERSE--CATEGORY III. ASSET INCREASE / ASSET DECREASE

Category	Class									
	Market Transactions		General Changes		Specific Changes		Forecast Changes		Conversion	
	A		B		C		D		E	
	Recorded	Rule	Recorded	Rule	Recorded	Rule	Recorded	Rule	Recorded	Rule
1. Physical - Physical	+	A-1	-	B	+	III-4	0		+	III-1
2. Physical - Legal	+	A-1 A-2	-	B	0		0		+	III-1
3. Physical - Economic	+	A-1	-	B	0		0		+	III-1
4. Legal - Physical	+	A-1	-	B	+	III-4	0		+	III-2
5. Legal - Legal	+	A-2	-	B	+	III-4	0		+	III-2
6. Legal - Economic	0		-	B	0		0		+	III-2
7. Economic - Physical	+	A-1	-	B	0		0		-	III-3
8. Economic - Legal	+	A-2	-	B	0		0		-	III-3
9. Economic - Economic	0		-	B	0		0		-	III-3

+ indicates the event is recorded
- indicates the event is not recorded
0 indicates the event does not exist
The letters and Roman numerals refer to the rules governing recognition.

Type III-A (2) Market transaction resulting in a physical asset increase / legal asset decrease

Example: The collection of receivables

Entry. -- Dr. Cash
Cr. Accounts Receivable

Accounting treatment. -- The event is recognized.

Applicable rules: A-1; A-2. -- The new asset (cash) qualifies under Rule I-1 and the inflow and outflow could be recorded separately. The event could therefore affect the residual equity. However, the inflow and outflow are identical and the event is recorded as an exchange.

Type III-A (3) Market transaction resulting in a physical asset increase / economic asset decrease

No event of this type exists.

Type III-A (4) Market transaction resulting in a legal asset increase / physical asset decrease

All exchanges of this type are recognized by recording the inflow and outflow separately.

Type III-A (5) Market transaction resulting in a legal asset increase / legal asset decrease

Example: The exchange of accounts receivable for notes receivable

Entry. -- Dr. Notes Receivable
Cr. Accounts Receivable

Accounting treatment. -- The event is recorded.

Applicable rule: A-2.

Type III-A (6) Market transaction resulting in a legal asset increase / economic asset decrease

No event of this type exists.

Type III-A (7) Market transactions resulting in an economic asset increase / physical asset decrease

Example: The purchase of good will

Entry. -- Dr. Good will

Cr. Cash

Accounting treatment. -- The event is recorded usually as part of a more complex transaction.

Applicable rule: A-1.

Type III-A (8, 9) Market transaction resulting in an economic asset increase / legal or economic asset

These events do not exist.

Type III-B (1, 2, 3, 4, 5, 6, 7, 8, 9) A general change resulting in an asset increase / asset decrease

These events do not exist. If they did exist, they could not be recorded because of Rule B.

Type III-C (1) A specific change resulting in a physical asset increase / physical asset decrease

Example: The destruction of an insured asset reimbursed by insurance proceeds

Entry. -- Dr. Cash

Cr. Building or inventory

Accounting treatment. -- The event is recorded.

Applicable rule: III-4. -- The event is recorded. Usually the destruction and subsequent reimbursement are recorded as separate events.

Type III-C (2, 3) A specific change resulting in a physical asset increase / legal or economic asset decrease

These events do not exist.

Type III-C (4) A specific change resulting in a legal asset increase / physical asset decrease

Example: The destruction of an insured asset

Entry. -- Dr. Due from Insurance Company
Cr. Building
or Inventory

Accounting treatment. -- The event is recorded.

Applicable rule: III-4.

Type III-C (5) A specific change resulting in a legal asset increase / legal asset decrease

Example 1: A receivable becomes uncollectible

Entry. -- Dr. Estimated Uncollectible Accounts
Cr. Accounts Receivable

Accounting treatment. -- The event is recognized as one of this type if an allowance system is used. If an allowance system is not used, the change is recognized as a Category II event.

Applicable rule: III-4.

Example 2: The receipt of pre-emptive stock rights

Entry. -- Dr. Investments - Rights
Cr. Investment - Stock

Accounting treatment. -- The event is recognized.

Applicable rules: I-3; C. -- Rule C demands that the receipt of stock rights be recorded. Rule I-3 prohibits the recognition of an asset increase as a result of this event and the event is recognized as a Category III event.

Type III-C (6) A specific change resulting in a legal asset increase / economic asset decrease

This event does not exist.

Type III-C (7, 8, 9) A specific change resulting in an economic asset increase / any asset decrease

No events of these types exist.

Type III-D (1, 2, 3, 4, 5, 6, 7, 8, 9) A forecast resulting in any asset increase / any asset decrease

No events of these types exist. It would have been possible to categorize the portion of the depreciation charge considered part of the manufactured product as an event of this type. The recognition of the accumulated depreciation is considered a forecast change. This forecast change can be recorded implicitly through a conversion. Recording the conversion by the entry:

Dr. Work in Process
Cr. Accumulated Depreciation

has the effect of reducing the depreciable asset to an amount reflecting the changed forecast about the life span. In this case, the conversion (a Class E event) implicitly records the forecast change. If no conversion is recorded, the forecast change is explicitly recorded as a Category II event. Thus, the depreciation is never recognized as a Type III-D event.

Type III-E (1) A conversion resulting in a physical asset increase / physical asset decrease

Example 1: The use of material in the manufacturing process

Entry. -- Dr. Work in Process
Cr. Raw Materials

Accounting treatment. -- The event must be recorded.

Applicable rule: III-1.

Example 2: The use of machines in the manufacturing process

Entry. -- Dr. Work in Process
Cr. Accumulated Depreciation

Accounting treatment. -- The event must be recorded.

Applicable rule: III-1. -- Rule III-1 states that a part of all costs relevant to the production process must be absorbed by each unit of product. Therefore "variable" or "relevant" costing is prohibited since under these costing methods units of inventory may or may not absorb fixed costs.

Type III-E (2) A conversion resulting in a physical asset increase / legal asset decrease

Example: The use of labor in the manufacturing process

Entry. -- Dr. Working Process
Cr. Labor Services

Accounting treatment. -- The event must be recorded.

Applicable rule: III-1.

Type III-E (3) A conversion resulting in a physical asset increase / economic asset decrease

The event does not exist.

Type III-E (4) A conversion resulting in a legal asset increase / physical asset decrease

Example: The use of material or machines in developing a patent

Entry. -- Dr. Patent
Cr. Raw Materials
or Accumulated Depreciation

<u>Accounting treatment</u>. -- The event may be recorded (it seldom is).

<u>Applicable rule: III-2</u>.

<u>Type III-E (5) A conversion resulting in a legal asset increase / legal asset decrease</u>

Example: The use of labor in developing a patent

<u>Entry</u>. -- Dr. Patent
Cr. Labor Services

<u>Accounting treatment</u>. -- The event may be recorded (it seldom is).

<u>Applicable rule: III-2</u>.

<u>Type III-E (6) A conversion resulting in a legal asset increase / economic asset decrease</u>

The event does not exist.

<u>Type III-E (7) A conversion resulting in an economic asset increase / physical asset decrease</u>

Example: The use of material or machines in research

<u>Entry</u>. -- Dr. Research
Cr. Raw Materials
or Accumulated Depreciation

<u>Accounting treatment</u>. -- The event is not recorded.

<u>Applicable rule: III-3</u>.

<u>Type III-E (8) A conversion resulting in an economic asset increase / legal asset decrease</u>

Example: The use of advertising services in developing customer good will

<u>Entry</u>. -- Dr. Customer Good will
Cr. Advertising Services

Accounting treatment. -- The event is not recorded.

Applicable rule: III-3.

Type III-E (9) A conversion resulting in an economic asset increase / economic asset decrease

The event does not exist.

Category IV

Type IV-A (1) Market transaction resulting in a specific equity increase / residual equity decrease

The entry does not exist.

Type IV-A (2) Market transaction resulting in a specific equity increase / specific equity decrease

Example: The exchange of bonds or preferred stock into common stock

Entry. -- Dr. Bonds
or Preferred Stock
Cr. Common Stock

Accounting treatment. -- The event is recorded.

Applicable rules: IV-1; A-2.

Type IV-A (3) Market transaction resulting in a residual equity increase / specific equity decrease

Example: The retirement of bonds at less than book value

Entry. -- Dr. Bonds Payable
Cr. Residual Equity

Accounting treatment. -- The event is recorded.

TABLE 8

ACCOUNTING UNIVERSE--CATEGORY IV. EQUITY INCREASE / EQUITY DECREASE

Category	Class									
	Market Transactions		General Changes		Specific Changes		Forecast Changes		Conversion	
	A		B		C		D		E	
	Recorded	Rule	Recorded	Rule	Recorded	Rule	Recorded	Rule	Recorded	Rule
1. Specific - Residual	0		-	B	+	C IV-1	+	IV-2 D-1	+	IV-1
2. Specific - Specific	+	IV-1	-	B	0		0		0	
3. Residual - Specific	+	IV-1	-	B	+	C IV-1	0		0	
4. Residual - Residual	0		-	B	0		0		0	

+ indicates the event is recorded
- indicates the event is not recorded
0 indicates the event does not exist
The letters and Roman numerals refer to the rules governing recognition.

Applicable rules: IV-1; A-2. -- This event is usually recorded as part of a compound entry as follows:

Dr. Bonds Payable

Cr. Cash
Cr. Residual Equity

Type IV-A (4) Market transaction resulting in a residual equity increase / residual equity decrease

Since there is only one residual equity, no such event can exist.

Type IV-B (1, 2, 3, 4) General changes resulting in an equity increase / equity decrease

Example: The value change in a liability due to general price level changes

Entry. -- Dr. or Cr. Bonds
Cr. or Dr. Residual Equity

Accounting treatment. -- The event is not recorded.

Applicable rule: B.

Type IV-C (1) A specific change resulting in a specific equity increase / residual equity decrease

Example: An unfavorable judgment in a law suit

Entry. -- Dr. Residual Equity
Cr. Payable

Accounting treatment. -- The event is recorded.

Applicable rules: C; IV-1.

Type IV-C (2) A specific change resulting in a specific equity increase / specific equity decrease

The event does not exist.

depreciation differs from tax depreciation, these benefits have different service paths. In that case, the amortization of the tax benefit represents a relative forecast change about the tax potential life and is recognize under Rule D-1.

Type IV-D (2) A forecast resulting in a specific equity increase / specific equity decrease

The event does not exist.

Type IV-D (3, 4) A forecast resulting in a residual equity increase / any equity decrease

These events do not exist.

Type IV-E (1) A conversion resulting in a specific equity increase / residual equity decrease

Example: The declaration of a dividend.

Entry. -- Dr. Residual Equity
Cr. Payable

Accounting treatment. -- The event is recorded.

Applicable rule: IV-1.

Type IV-E (2, 3, 4) Conversions resulting in equity increase / equity decreases

The events do not exist.

CHAPTER VII

CONCLUSION AND IMPLICATIONS

This paper has examined the selection process of accounting. Assets and equities have been defined and a framework for organizing accounting events has been suggested. Based on the proposed framework, the accounting events were grouped into classes and categories. The selection rules appropriate to these classes and categories were then derived and tested. Hopefully, this study will serve as a springboard for further investigations. The preceding analyses certainly suggest some of the major areas that require further attention. Among these are: the influence of auditability, the restatement of accounting concepts, and the organizational framework.

The influence of auditability

Is there any logical connection between the eighteen selection rules derived and tested in the previous chapter? Even a cursory examination of the rules establishes the central influence that auditability or verifiability exercises upon the rules. The influence of auditability asserts itself in the following biases displayed by the rules. (1) A bias for recording physical and legal changes. (2) A bias toward recording events that can be described, even if only arbitrarily, by means of a single valued number or a point estimate. The rules suggest a corresponding bias against recording events that can adequately be described only through two or more numbers, i.e., a distribution. (3) A bias for recording enduring and/or predictable changes. Accounting prefers the tangible to the intangible; a single number to a range and the arbitrary to the relative.

Rules A-1, A-2, C, I-3, III-1, III-2, VI-1 exhibit the bias towards recording physical and legal changes. Rules I-1, II, III-1, and III-4 indicate a preference twoard recording events describable by a single number. Rule I-1 insists that a reasonable quantification is contained within the asset itself. Rule III-1 assigns an equal share of production costs to each unit produced, whether sold or inventoried, and thus one single figure describes each unit of output with no questions asked. Rule II, Rule III-3, and Rule D-1 indicate accountings preference toward recording enduring and predictable changes.

These biases are easy to rationalize on the basis of auditability. Physical and legal changes are easily verified and hard to ignore. What is an auditor to do if he stubs his toe on an unrecorded physical asset? Does he not bruise?

Single valued descriptions, and especially single valued descriptions of "zero," are clearly preferable. It is easier to verify or reject a single number than a distribution. If the single number is zero, the event resulting in such a change is generally irreversible. If the effects of an event are enduring, they may be audited at any time. If the effects are fleeting, verification must pertain to the short period of time during which the effects persisted. The same may be said of predictable changes. All of the relative forecast changes recognized by accounting are completely predictable. The entires recording these changes could be prepared and audited at any time during the life of the asset or equity.

One caveat, about the influence of auditability must be mentioned. A "verification fallacy" may well exist. Physical changes can be verified more easily than economic changes. The existence of physical assets can be established more easily than the existence of economic assets. It is generally agreed that accounting is concerned with economic events and economic data. In the last analysis, it must always be economic changes and economic assets that need to be audited and confirmed. Does the verification of physical changes also result in verifying the associated economic change? Does the verification of the existence of a physical or legal asset, also verify the existence of the economic asset? It is here that the "verification fallacy" may well lie, if accounting feels that the verification of the physical appearance also verifies the economic substance. "Accounting is concerned with economic attributes and measurements, not with physical layout as such."[1] Auditing must audit economic attributes and it remains a moot point whether economic attributes having a physical or legal manifestation can be effectively audited through a verification of the physical or legal manifestation.

No one questions the important role that auditability should play in the selection process. However, it seems like putting the cart before the horse to insist that no event should be recorded unless it is easily auditable. Furthermore, this type of view sells the auditors ingenuity and genius short. If events are recorded, the auditor will find appropriate and effective auditing techniques.

The restatement of accounting concepts

The rules that have been derived make it possible to restate accounting concepts in terms of operational rules unburdened by emotional connotations. Each rule can then be analyzed, discussed, and evaluated precisely and dispassionately. Given the existing ambiguously and imprecisely stated accounting principles, this is something that is currently impossible.

---

[1] W.A. Paton and A.C. Littleton, An Introduction to Corporate Accounting Standards (Columbus: American Accounting Association, 1955), pp. 13-14.

The organizational framework

Although the search for a unifying theory underlying accounting, and the operational expression of what accounting actually does, can and hopefully will lead to useful results, perhaps the most rewarding potential of the study lies in the classification scheme adopted. The particular classes and categories of events selected are unimportant, but the definition of the subject matter of accounting as events, and the grouping of these events into classes and categories is important. The benefit of this approach is twofold; viewing accounting as events does not restrict one to "either/or" judgments. In *A Theory of Accounting for Investors*, Staubus, for instance, devotes a good portion of chapter iii discussing *the* proper valuation base for different assets.[1] Selection of one base implies the rejection of another. If value changes are thought of as events, then the "either/or problem" disappears. Market transactions and value changes can both be recorded or rejected; the selection of one does not imply the rejection of the other.

These events can, if appropriate, be described and communicated by distinct and different methods, which leads to the second potential benefit of this or a similar classification scheme. In this study five different classes of events, twenty-five different categories of events, and a hundred and twenty-five types of events were discussed. Accounting deals with many varied events. If a classification scheme is based on valid differences between classes and categories, this suggests that a different measurement techniques, different communicating devices, different selection rules, even different auditing criteria and standards might be appropriate for the different classes and categories of events. It suggests the possibility that one and only one system of description,

---

[1] George Staubus, *A Theory of Accounting to Investors* (Berkeley: University of California Press, 1961), chapter iii.

selection, and communication might be inadequate. The valid criticism has often been laid against accounting that it adds "apples" and "oranges." But that does not mean that one may not eat both. This does not mean that accounting should be concerned only with either "apples" or "oranges." Both might very well be the proper subject matter of accounting. All different types of events might properly be the subject matter of accounting. The error lies not in dealing with different events but in commingling these events, and in insisting that the proper treatment for one type of event is necessarily the proper treatment for all.

Conclusion

The main purpose of this paper will have been service if additional insight has been gained about current accounting practices. If it is true that "the child is father of the man," then knowledge about the child should aid in the development of the man. This paper represents an attempt to understand accounting as it now is, in order to help it develop into what it should become.

BIBLIOGRAPHY

American Accounting Association. Accounting and Reporting Standards for Corporate Financial Statements and Preceding Statements and Supplements. Columbus: American Accounting Association, 1957.

American Institute of Certified Public Accountants. Review and Resumé, Bulletin, No. 1. New York: American Institute of Certified Public Accountants, 1953.

________. Accounting Research Bulletin No. 43. New York: American Institute of Certified Public Accountants, 1953.

Anton, Hector R. "Accounting for Bond Liabilities," The Journal of Accountancy, Vol. CII (September, 1956).

Bierman, Harold, Jr., and Green, David, Jr. "Accounting for Income Taxes -- The Problems Arising from Certificates of Necessity," The Federal Accountants, VI (June, 1957), 30-34.

Canning, John B. The Economics of Accountancy. New York: The Ronald Press Company, 1929.

Davidson, Sidney. "Accelerated Depreciation and the Allocation of Income Taxes," The Accounting Review, XXXII (April, 1958), 173-80.

Devine, Carl. Inventory Valuation and Periodic Income. New York: The Ronald Press Company, 1942.

Gilman, Stephen. Accounting Concepts of Profit. New York: The Ronald Press Company, 1939.

Green, David, Jr. "Accounting for Corporate Retained Earnings." Unpublished Ph.D. dissertation, Graduate School of Business, University of Chicago, 1956.

_____. "A Moral to the Direct Costing Controversy," The Journal of Business, XXXIII (July, 1960), 218-26.

Green, David, Jr., and Sorter, George H. "Accounting for Obsolescence -- A Proposal," The Accounting Review, XXXIV (July, 1959), 433-41.

Kester, Roy B. Accounting Theory and Practice. New York: The Ronald Press Company, 1921.

Marple, Raymond F. Capital Surplus and Corporate Networth. New York: The Ronald Press Company, 1936.

Paton, W.A. Essentials of Accounting. New York: The Macmillan Company, 1938.

Paton, W.A., and Paton, W.A., Jr. Asset Accounting. New York: The Macmillan Company, 1952.

Paton, W.A., and Littleton, A.C. An Introduction to Corporate Accounting Standards. Columbus: American Accounting Association, 1955.

Pearson, Karl. The Grammar of Science. New York: The Meridian Books, Inc. 1957.

Rorem, C. Rufus. Accounting Method. Chicago: University of Chicago Press, 1930.

Rowbury, James, Jr. "Timber Depletion," The Accounting Review XXII (April, 1947), 188-89.

Shillinglaw, Gordon. "Leasing and Financial Statements," The Accounting Review, XXXIII (October, 1958), 581-92.

Sorter, George H., and Horngren, Charles T. "Asset Recognition and Economic Attributes -- The Relevant Costing Approach," The Accounting Review, XXXVII (July, 1962), 391-99.

Staubus, George. A Theory of Accounting to Investors. Berkeley: University of California Press, 1961.

Vatter, William J. The Fund Theory of Accounting and Its Implication for Financial Reports. Chicago: University of Chicago Press, 1947.

Wixon, Rufus (ed.). Accountants' Handbook. 4th ed. New York: The Ronald Press Company, 1956.

Yntema, Theodore O. "Discussion of Literature," Publication of the American Association of University Instructors in Accounting, IX (February, 1925), 62.

Zizes, Alvin. "Disclosure of Long Term Leases," The Journal of Accountancy, CXI (February, 1961), 37-47.

THE DEVELOPMENT OF CONTEMPORARY ACCOUNTING THOUGHT

An Arno Press Collection

Baldwin, H[arry] G[len]. **Accounting for Value As Well as Original Cost** *and* Castenholz, William B. **A Solution to the Appreciation Problem.** 2 Vols. in 1. 1927/1931

Baxter, William. **Collected Papers on Accounting.** 1978

Brief, Richard P., Ed. **Selections from Encyclopaedia of Accounting, 1903.** 1978

Broaker, Frank and Richard M. Chapman. **The American Accountants' Manual.** 1897

Canning, John B. **The Economics of Accountancy.** 1929

Chatfield, Michael, Ed. **The English View of Accountant's Duties and Responsibilities.** 1978

Cole, William Morse. **The Fundamentals of Accounting.** 1921

Congress of Accountants. **Official Record of the Proceedings of the Congress of Accountants.** 1904

Cronhelm, F[rederick] W[illiam]. **Double Entry by Single.** 1818

Davidson, Sidney. **The Plant Accounting Regulations of the Federal Power Commission.** 1952

De Paula, F[rederic] R[udolf] M[ackley]. **Developments in Accounting.** 1948

Epstein, Marc Jay. **The Effect of Scientific Management on the Development of the Standard Cost System** (Doctoral Dissertation, University of Oregon, 1973). 1978

Esquerré, Paul-Joseph. **The Applied Theory of Accounts.** 1914

Fitzgerald, A[dolf] A[lexander]. **Current Accounting Trends.** 1952

Garner, S. Paul and Marilynn Hughes, Eds. **Readings on Accounting Development.** 1978

Haskins, Charles Waldo. **Business Education and Accountancy.** 1904

Hein, Leonard William. **The British Companies Acts and the Practice of Accountancy 1844-1962** (Doctoral Dissertation, University of California, Los Angeles, 1962). 1978

Hendriksen, Eldon S. **Capital Expenditures in the Steel Industry, 1900 to 1953** (Doctoral Dissertation, University of California, Berkeley, 1956). 1978

Holmes, William, Linda H. Kistler and Louis S. Corsini. **Three Centuries of Accounting in Massachusetts.** 1978

Horngren, Charles T. **Implications for Accountants of the Uses of Financial Statements by Security Analysts** (Doctoral Dissertation, University of Chicago, 1955). 1978

Horrigan, James O., Ed. **Financial Ratio Analysis—An Historical Perspective.** 1978

Jones, [Edward Thomas]. **Jones's English System of Book-keeping.** 1796

Lamden, Charles William. **The Securities and Exchange Commission** (Doctoral Dissertation, University of California, Berkeley, 1949). 1978

Langer, Russell Davis. **Accounting As A Variable in Mergers** (Doctoral Dissertation, University of California, Berkeley, 1976). 1978

Lewis, J. Slater. **The Commercial Organisation of Factories.** 1896

Littleton, A[nanias] C[harles] and B[asil] S. Yamey, Eds. **Studies in the Historv of Accounting.** 1956

Mair, John. **Book-keeping Moderniz'd.** 1793

Mann, Helen Scott. **Charles Ezra Sprague.** 1931

Marsh, C[hristopher] C[olumbus]. **The Theory and Practice of Bank Book-keeping.** 1856

Mitchell, William. **A New and Complete System of Book-keeping by an Improved Method of Double Entry.** 1796

Montgomery, Robert H. **Fifty Years of Accountancy.** 1939

Moonitz, Maurice. **The Entity Theory of Consolidated Statements.** 1951

Moonitz, Maurice, Ed. **Three Contributions to the Development of Accounting Thought.** 1978

Murray, David. **Chapters in the History of Bookkeeping, Accountancy & Commercial Arithmetic.** 1930

Nicholson, J[erome] Lee. **Cost Accounting.** 1913

Paton, William Andrew and Russell Alger Stevenson. **Principles of Accounting.** 1918

Pixley, Francis W[illiam]. **The Profession of a Chartered Accountant and Other Lectures.** 1897

Preinreich, Gabriel A. D. **The Nature of Dividends.** 1935

Previts, Gary John, Ed. **Early 20th Century Developments in American Accounting Thought.** 1978

Ronen, Joshua and George H. Sorter. **Relevant Financial Statements.** 1978

Shenkir, William G., Ed. **Carman G. Blough: His Professional Career and Accounting Thought.** 1978

Simpson, Kemper. **Economics for the Accountant.** 1921

Sneed, Florence R. **Parallelism in Two Disciplines.** (M.A. Thesis, University of Texas, Arlington, 1974). 1978

Sorter, George H. **The Boundaries of the Accounting Universe** (Doctoral Dissertation, University of Chicago, 1963). 1978

Storey, Reed K[arl]. **Matching Revenues with Costs** (Doctoral Dissertation, University of California, Berkeley, 1958). 1978

Sweeney, Henry W[hitcomb]. **Stabilized Accounting.** 1936

Van de Linde, Gérard. **Reminiscences.** 1917

Vatter, William J[oseph]. **The Fund Theory of Accounting and Its Implications for Financial Reports.** 1947

Walker, R. G. **Consolidated Statements.** 1978

Webster, Norman E., Comp. **The American Association of Public Accountants.** 1954

Wells, M. C., Ed. **American Engineers' Contributions to Cost Accounting.** 1978

Worthington, Beresford. **Professional Accountants.** 1895

Yamey, Basil S. **Essays on the History of Accounting.** 1978

Yamey, Basil S., Ed. **The Historical Development of Accounting.** 1978

Yang, J[u] M[ei]. **Goodwill and Other Intangibles.** 1927

Zeff, Stephen Addam. **A Critical Examination of the Orientation Postulate in Accounting, with Particular Attention to its Historical Development** (Doctoral Dissertation, University of Michigan, 1961). 1978

Zeff, Stephen A., Ed. **Selected Dickinson Lectures in Accounting.** 1978